I am bored and I am TIRED of it!!

Monique Myers, LCSW

BALBOA
PRESS
A DIVISION OF HAY HOUSE

Copyright © 2014 Monique Myers, LCSW.

All rights reserved. No part of this book may be used or reproduced by any means, graphic, electronic, or mechanical, including photocopying, recording, taping or by any information storage retrieval system without the written permission of the publisher except in the case of brief quotations embodied in critical articles and reviews.

Balboa Press books may be ordered through booksellers or by contacting:

Balboa Press
A Division of Hay House
1663 Liberty Drive
Bloomington, IN 47403
www.balboapress.com
1 (877) 407-4847

Because of the dynamic nature of the Internet, any web addresses or links contained in this book may have changed since publication and may no longer be valid. The views expressed in this work are solely those of the author and do not necessarily reflect the views of the publisher, and the publisher hereby disclaims any responsibility for them.

The author of this book does not dispense medical advice or prescribe the use of any technique as a form of treatment for physical, emotional, or medical problems without the advice of a physician, either directly or indirectly. The intent of the author is only to offer information of a general nature to help you in your quest for emotional and spiritual well-being. In the event you use any of the information in this book for yourself, which is your constitutional right, the author and the publisher assume no responsibility for your actions.

Any people depicted in stock imagery provided by Thinkstock are models, and such images are being used for illustrative purposes only.
Certain stock imagery © Thinkstock.

Printed in the United States of America.

ISBN: 978-1-4525-9711-9 (sc)
ISBN: 978-1-4525-9713-3 (hc)
ISBN: 978-1-4525-9712-6 (e)

Library of Congress Control Number: 2014907874

Balboa Press rev. date: 5/16/2014

Contents

Introduction		vii
Chapter 1	Definitions	1
Chapter 2	Boredom, Depression, or Midlife Crisis	21
Chapter 3	Boredom and Eating, Relationships, Children, and Addiction	40
Chapter 4	Boredom and Acknowledgment and Hobbies	56
Chapter 5	My Experiences with Personal Responsibility	64
Chapter 6	Taking Responsibility for Your Life	71
Chapter 7	Why You May Not Be Taking Responsibility for Your Life	77
Chapter 8	What Can Occur If You Do Not Take Responsibility for Your Life	84
Chapter 9	How You Can Take Responsibility for Your Life	97

Introduction

Oftentimes you may look at your life and think about the could have, would have, and should haves ... and wonder why—why you have not done this or that, why you treated people a certain way, why people have treated you a certain way, why you continue to do the same thing over and over, why you stay in an unhealthy relationship, why your children act out, why you are overweight, why you sit on the couch instead of walking and exercising, why you drink too much, why you are unhappy, why you are bored, why you didn't finish school ... why, why, why! You ask yourself questions that only you can answer. Some questions never get answered, which can cause frustration with yourself and others. Instead of asking yourself why, ask yourself how, how can I change, how can I react to this situation, how can I make sure it does not happen again, how can I stop being bored.

You may feel bored with your life—at times, even hopeless regarding your future—due to feeling you *can't* live the life you want to live. Well, I am here to tell you that life does not have to be boring or difficult. You don't have to continue to ask yourself, *Why, why, why* all the time and get yourself discouraged. If you are like me—and I am sure you are, due to your picking out this book—you have asked yourself, why does life have to be so unfulfilling? That is a question that I and so many others continue to ask. As a woman who has approached the ripe old age of fortysomething and who has also been a social worker for over twenty years, I have found that many people are miserable and unhappy with their lives. It doesn't matter if they are young or old; male or female;

rich or poor; white, black, brown, or purple; with children or without children; married or unmarried; employed or unemployed, people overall just continue to have a hard time figuring out what they want in their life and how to feel happy and content.

There are many, many reasons why people are not happy and satisfied with their lives, but what I keep hearing is that they are bored with their lives; that they don't know what to do with themselves; that they aren't happy with their relationships, with their children, with their jobs—basically, with their lives. Even though people are busier than ever and have a thousand things to do, they are still bored and unhappy. Even with all the technology and electronics at our disposal, we find ourselves bored. I am not saying that everyone is bored and miserable, but think about a time in your life when you were not happy or content—what was occurring in your life, and what were you doing or not doing during that time? That moment might be right now, or it might have been years ago. Most of the time we know what is making us unhappy, but we have a hard time either admitting it or dealing with it, which causes us to feel "stuck", hopeless or miserable. Throughout this book I will ask you several questions and I want you to be mindful, yes mindful, of what your actually thinking and feelings. While reading this book, I want you to be in the moment and allow yourself to process what you are thinking and feeling. So when I ask you to think about a time when you felt unhappy or discontented in your life, what is the first thought that comes to your mind? This thought might lead to thinking of a situation or a person in your life. You may have thoughts of being uncertain about your future—the unknown—or you may be grieving the loss of someone or something. You may feel you cannot change a situation that you are in. Sometimes you really don't know what is going on until you are able to ask yourself some tough question and process what you are thinking and feeling. I am not saying that every time you are unhappy, you are bored, but I do want you to be able to identify the reason for your unhappiness and the reasons that may cause you to act or feel in a certain way.

Ask yourself, when do I feel my best? When do I feel my worst? Getting inside your own mind and identifying your feelings and thoughts is the first step to understanding and identifying the reasons for your actions and behaviors. Your thoughts, positive or negative, are the key to your happiness or unhappiness. For example, if you continue to have positive thoughts and a positive outlook on life, you will most likely be a happy, content person. You will have a good outlook on life and be able to handle any situation that is thrown your way. However, if you have negative, irrational thoughts or a negative outlook on life, you will perceive your life as hopeless and will not be able to handle situations. This, in turn, will cause you to act negatively or to do nothing to correct your situation. Doing something that is irrational and unhealthy or not doing anything at all both can be negative actions. These negative actions may have been fueled by your feelings or irrational thoughts. Again, the first step to making positive changes in your life is taking responsibility for your thoughts and making a conscious effort to change your negative thoughts.

Now, making changes in your thought process takes time—it will not happen overnight. If your thoughts have been negative for a long time, it will take a long time to train your brain to think positively. You will basically have to "rewire" your brain. I hope that by the time you have finished reading this book, you will have had enough time to change your negative thoughts and being "bored" to having positive thoughts and giving your life purpose and meaning. You will feel a sense of purpose and fulfillment when you take charge of your thoughts, actions, and life; hopefully you will start living the life that you want to live.

There are several reasons why we have irrational thoughts that cause us to act certain ways, but I want to focus on how boredom—yes, boredom—affects people's lives and causes negative thoughts, actions, and choices and often leads to self-destructive behaviors. I will share personal thoughts and experiences in this book so that you can understand how changing my thought process has helped me through the difficult times.

Over the past couple of years, I have questioned myself regarding my purpose in this world. I have had that unsettled feeling that there is more to life than what I have been living. After evaluating myself, I found that when I get bored with my life and do not feel there is any direction, I get antsy, frustrated, angry, and depressed. I don't like myself, and I like to blame everyone else for *my* negative feelings and *my* miserable life. My life is far from miserable, but at times, it does feel like there is nothing good about it. As a clinical social worker I often find myself feeling the same way as my client's bored and confused, I am human, and I do go through the same feelings and difficulties as my clients. I have found that helping others also helps me to understand and take a new perspective of what I may be going through.

So let me tell you a little about myself: I am a forty year old (*oh my God!*) married woman who works full-time. I take care of my mother, who has Alzheimer's, and my eighteen-year-old niece. I have a dog, a cat, five fish, and a house that I have to clean and make comfy and cozy. I go to work every day, give my job 100 percent, and at times, I leave work feeling empty. I try to exercise every day, and I like doing fun activities, but I still managed to feel bored. I even found myself getting bored while running—don't know how this happened, but it did and at times still does. So I began to ask myself, what is wrong with me? I have heard it said, "If you are bored, then you are boring." Is this true? I never considered myself a boring person, but I started to wonder, is the reason I am bored is because I am a boring person? I have always liked being around people who entertain me and looking back on my life, I have always depended on others to make decisions about what we are going to do. So the question is raised again: am I a boring person or am I just not taking responsibility for my life? I hate to think I am a boring person, but I ask myself this question more and more: am I *boring, boring, boring*? Is this boredom a lack of happiness, or is it depression, or is it a midlife crisis? Is it that I am not being true to what I really think and want? By evaluating my life and asking myself some tough questions I have been able to recognize that by taking control of *my* life, *my* thought, feelings and actions and making *myself* happy I can eliminate boredom and have a life with purpose and meaning.

My hope for writing this book is to help you recognize why you are having boredom and negative thoughts about your life and what *you* can do to make your life better. In this book, I will ramble on and on about why you may be feeling bored and how this affects daily life. I will also focus on how personal responsibility and boredom have positive and negative effects on your life and what you can do to have a more fulfilling, exciting, and happier existence in this crazy world. I will try to help you assess and make changes within your relationships, employment, and personal activities that will enhance a healthier, happier you.

Writing this book has allowed me to vent my feelings with regard to people not taking personal responsibility. These are *my* feelings, thoughts and opinions. I am being truthful about what I have experienced and what I have witnessed others doing or not doing on the topic of boredom and personal responsibility and how they relate to one another. I do not always take full responsibility for every one of my actions or thoughts, but I take care of myself physically, emotionally, and spiritually. I take care of my finances and make sure I can pay my bills and buy groceries. I also take care of my marital relationship, my friendships, and my family. Again, I am not here to judge anyone, but I can tell you from experience that not taking responsibility for your actions, thoughts, and emotions and not knowing who you are or what you want from yourself and others, and not being able to deal with the consequences from your actions and thoughts can lead you to a life of boredom, loneliness, sadness, regret, and destructive behaviors.

Chapter 1

Definitions

The cure for boredom is curiosity. There is no cure for curiosity.
—Dorothy Parker

I have become more and more frustrated and disappointed with how people treat one another and how they are not held accountable for their thoughts and actions. When I've discussed this with other professionals and with friends and family, it is clear that we all feel the same way. As a licensed clinical social worker, I work daily with individuals who have difficulties in life and who are struggling with moving forward in their lives. They report feeling stuck, unhappy, unmotivated, bored and confused. I have found myself having these same feeling and thoughts and started to ask myself "what am I doing to get me through these times when I do not feel my best, when I myself am struggling with life?" At times, I find it difficult to give advice to those who are needing guidance, when I have a hard time following my own advice and guidance. Still, I will say this one to a thousand times: I am not perfect, and I do not have all the answers, but I do try to help myself and others by recognizing my faults and making changes that need to be made. Most of the time when I am not truthful with myself and do not take personal responsibility for my actions and thoughts, I find myself bored, tired, depressed, sad, selfish, and angry at everyone else (because in my mind, they are the problem). I have realized, however, that *I* am causing these issues and problems, due to my negative thoughts, choices and behaviors. I have tried to "talk the talk and walk the walk" and I have to say it has made my life healthier, happier and better.

I have found that when people are unhappy, they are unable to understand or recognize that it is not their parents', spouse's, boyfriend/girlfriend's, children's, families, friend's, coworker's, boss's, or neighbor's fault for their life's misfortune; it is their own fault. When your life is spiraling out of control, you need to point the finger at yourself and ask, "What am I doing to cause these problems?" I have found that self-reflection does not happen as much as it should. I feel that people blame everyone and everything else for their misfortunes, instead of looking at themselves and asking, "Why is this happening and how can I change it?"

There is not one particular situation or person to blame regarding why people are not taking responsibility for their lives. It is a combination of generation after generation of parents wanting their children to have a better life than they had, parents wanting to be friends with their child instead of a parent, parents afraid to be parents due to society judging or criticizing them, government programs handing out money and services to those who are not working or taking care of their needs, materialistic thought processes ("gotta have it" attitudes), insurance liability lawsuits, inconsistent expectations of others, and of course the wonderful news, Internet, and social media.

Society accepts all of the chaos and drama that fills the television, news, Internet, and social networks. We entertain this type of behavior and encourage it. I love to watch reality shows, just like most people, but I do not allow these shows to dictate my actions. I don't watch *Housewives* or *Kardashians* and think that I can act like them. I am able to understand that this is TV, and even though it is a "reality show," it is not real. There are a significant number of people, mostly adolescents, who are unable to recognize that what they see on TV is not real. This is causing our society to change and shift into a mentality that it is "ok" to be loud, annoying, disrespectful to others, it is "ok" to not work, it is "ok" to not have a good education, "it is "ok" to have 3 and 4 children with different men and not be married, it is "ok" to be self-centered and only care about yourself, it is "ok" to use people for what you want, it is "ok" to not take responsibility for your life, behavior and actions, it is "ok" not to do anything productive with your life, but is it really "ok"? The direction I see our society going worries me and makes me think it is not "ok". We have to make a change not only for ourselves but for those around us.

The first part of knowing how to make change is understanding what needs to be changed and then finding a way to make a change that works for you. I will define and give examples of what I mean when I use the words *boredom, responsibility, choices, actions, consequences, expectations, acceptance,* and *accountability.* I will ask you questions after each definition, and I want you to be honest with yourself when you answer them. Honesty is the key; if you are unable to be honest with yourself, you will never have self-fulfillment. Being honest with yourself can be a difficult challenge, especially if you are not used to focusing on yourself and listening to your intuition. When I tell people that they need to be honest with themselves, they often look at me like I am crazy. Some even get offended, because they feel they have been honest. But as you answer the questions, ask yourself if you are really being honest with yourself, or if you are answering the questions the way you *think* you should—the way you *think* others would want you to.

Being honest with yourself can be difficult, but it will get to the root of your problems. So you might ask yourself, "How can I know if I am truly being honest with myself when I answer these questions?" Well, when you ask yourself a question, you usually can answer quickly in your mind. I always suggest that the first thought that comes to mind is usually the truth. But there are times when you answer the question with another question, or you hesitate, or you answer it and then wonder if that answer was correct. It is in that moment that you have to ask yourself if you are being honest. Listen to your immediate inner thought, your intuition.

There are no right or wrong answers to any questions in this book. These questions merely gives you a chance to be completely honest with yourself without feeling judged or ashamed.

For example, do you smoke cigarettes? This might seem like a yes-or-no question, but for many, this will be difficult to answer. There are several ways that you might answer this question:

1. You answer immediately and confidently, with a yes or no.
2. You hesitate and ask yourself the question several times, pondering.
3. You answer with a *maybe, I don't know, not sure,* rationalizing your answer. For example, "I only smoke when I am with my friends who smoke."
4. You answer it yes or no but then rethink the question, and question if you do or don't.

Again, this question requires only a yes-or-no answer, and there is no right or wrong answer, but it is a question that you have to answer honestly, especially if you want to stop smoking.

If you are being completely honest with yourself, you will be able to answer the question immediately and with confidence. If you do hesitate, it should not be for long. If you are not sure or don't know and have to think about the answer for a long time, you may not be being honest with yourself. You may be trying to sway yourself to believe what you want to believe. Meanwhile, your gut is telling you the absolute truth. If the answer is, "Yes, I smoke cigarettes and I want to stop," then the first step has been completed: you have acknowledged the problem. You can move to the second step of moving forward with change.

As you read the questions in this book, I would like you to write out the answers and read them back to yourself. Again, there is no right or wrong answer to these questions. This is a way to help *you* understand yourself better and work on issues that you may be having and you want to change.

You will read certain words over and over again that I feel are important to define and explain. I want you to understand my definition of these words as I use them in this book so that there will be clear communication and understanding as you apply them to your daily thoughts, actions, and life.

Boredom: I want to clarify a misconception about boredom. Boredom is not just a thought or an action; it is a feeling. So when I ask you if you are feeling bored, ask yourself, "What am I feeling?" Usually, with the feeling of boredom comes restlessness, confusion, sadness, fear, depression, or hopelessness—basically, negative feelings; the feelings you don't want to acknowledge and get help for. We may be quick to tell someone, "I am sad" or "I am depressed," when in actuality, we may be bored. If you are unable to identify your true feeling, you will most likely focus on the wrong feeling, which does not allow you to fix the underlining feeling. (Wow, that was a mouthful!) Basically, if you go to a therapist and say you are feeling depressed, the therapist may focus on your statement that you are depressed and not the underlying feeling that you are actually bored and need help with your boredom, not depression. For example, a gentleman came to my office, stating that he was severely depressed. After discussing his depression for ten minutes, he was able to acknowledge that he was lonely and bored due to not having companionship. Once we were able to identify his true feeling, of loneliness and boredom, which were making him feel sad and hopeless we were able to identify ways to help with his boredom and loneliness. He left the session more hopeful about his life and focused on ways to meet other people and interact with them. He felt more hopeful and focused on ways to help relieve his sadness, by making the choices to make an effort to socialize with others and stop being bored and lonely. Today, he has stopped taking anti-depressants and is dating, working and making the life he envisioned.

Boredom is an <u>emotional</u> state, experienced when an individual is left without anything in particular to do and is not interested in his or her surroundings. So instead of focusing on sadness and depression, focus on your boredom and what is making you bored and what you can do to alleviate this boredom. For example, you may sit home on a Friday night and feel bored. You may feel restless due to not having nothing to do. You may feel lonely, sad for yourself, angry, or just blah. You can make a decision right then to do something to alleviate this boredom, such as exercise, go out to dinner, call a friend, watch a good movie, or do an arts-and-craft activity—or you can just sit there and be bored. If you decide to just sit there and be bored, your boredom is going to get worse. Therefore, the negative feelings associated with boredom could manifest. You have the choice to not be bored, which could elevate the negative feelings and thoughts you continue to have. (Wow, the choice of not being bored—what a nice concept.) There is a huge difference between boredom and depression, even though they may make you *feel* the same.

Questions I want you to think about:
(You can ask yourself these questions now or during a time when you feel restless, sad, or lonely.)

1. Am I bored?
2. With what am I bored?
3. With whom am I bored?
4. What can I do right now that will cause me not to be bored? (I want you to do whatever you thought of and recognize how you felt during and after doing it.)

Being bored is not always a bad thing. Sometimes I want to be bored and "veg out" on the couch and not think. I want to have time by myself and not have anything to do. When I do lie on the couch, I often find myself feeling guilty about it, but I have realized that at times, being bored and having nothing to do allows me to recharge my battery and become more creative and more focused. If I allow myself a day or two of being bored, usually the next day I have more energy, and I can focus on my goals with more purpose. So being bored can be instrumental in your life. When this boredom lasts for a long time, starts to consume your life, and causes negative issues to occur, however, that is when boredom is no longer beneficial and can become self-destructive.

Responsibility: A lot of people do not like to hear this word; they are confused on the definition. People usually think when someone says they need to take "responsibility" for their lives that he or she is judging them or putting them down. They may think the person is saying that they are not taking care of themselves or their families. People can become very defensive when discussing taking responsibility for their lives, but I have realized that people do not understand what "personal responsibility" means. Taking personal responsibility can help improve your life in so many ways. I feel that some people are not taking responsibility for their lives; therefore, there is more poverty, violence, depression, obesity, substance abuse and co-dependency than ever before. How can we stop this epidemic of negativity? My thought is that when you take personal responsibility, you take responsibility for *your* life. You take care of yourself, your family, and your needs. You take responsibility for the positive and negative consequences that may occur by your behaviors, and you take control of your reactions and feelings toward others. As the Dalai Lama stated, "To live a fulfilled life you have to live by the three Rs—respect for self, respect for others, and responsibility for all your actions."

There are several definitions of responsibility, but the one on which I specifically want to focus is personal responsibility—taking responsibility for the choices and actions that *you* make every day in *your* life and accepting that you are responsible for what you choose to feel and think. What does that mean? We, as individuals, are unique, one from the other, and we all feel and think differently. We all have different opinions, advice and thoughts. That is the beauty of being different, but I noticed over the years that people do not respect each other's differences, opinions and choices. Everyone, I mean everyone, has the right to their *own* thoughts, feelings, opinions and choices, and we need to respect that. We need to take responsibility for *our* own thoughts, feelings and behavior and not focus so much on how other's perceive or think about you. If you want to have negative thoughts all the time, you will have negative feelings and actions. If you are constantly dependent on what others think and feel about you, you will be emotionally drained and dependent on others. We all like to ask others for their opinions or directions when facing choices, but you need to realize that *you* make the final decision. Answer the following questions right now, as honestly as you can:

1. Based on the above definition, am I taking responsibility for my thoughts today?
2. Am I taking responsibility for my actions today?
3. Do I usually have positive or negative thoughts about my life?
4. What is one thing I can do differently to take responsibility for my life?

When you take responsibility for your life, you also *accept* the choices you have made. You are willing to say, "Yes, I did that," even if you know you will have negative consequences. You can't use the "yes, I did that, but ..." excuse. You have to admit that your action was wrong and be ready to take responsibility for it. Another aspect of personal responsibility is being able to *accept* yourself for who you are and to know what you want for yourself and your loved ones. It is important to know yourself and accept your limitations and strengths. It is also important to know and accept the person with whom you share your life with. In taking personal responsibility for your life, you also have to accept the people with whom you associate, fall in love, and spend time with. If you are in a relationship, you need to ask yourself what you can and cannot accept in your partner. This allows you to take responsibility for your relationship and ultimately will allow you to have a healthy relationship. By accepting another person's good and bad traits, you are saying, "I don't like this about you, but I can accept this." Being accepting of behaviors can also be beneficial when raising children or helping family members.

My niece has shown some behaviors that I don't like and feel are not good behaviors, but I accept that she is a teenager and is acting in a way that allows her to figure out who she is. I still accept her and love her as my niece, but I also allow her to learn and grow. I will discuss with her what I see her doing that I don't like, but I try not to put her down or make her feel ashamed about her behavior. Now that she is eighteen years old, I simply explain that I have concerns about her behavior but that she is an adult and will have to learn from her mistakes. I explain that I will love her no matter what she does, but she will have consequences for her actions. So far, talking to her about my concerns, having open communication and treating her with respect has helped her understand the concept of personal responsibility, which I hope will continue into her adulthood. Even though I see behavior I don't' "like" does not mean I don't "like" her. The same concept with my husband, there are behaviors that he shows that I have a hard time with but I asked myself years ago if I could accept them and I made the conscious decision that I could accept these behaviors even though I don't like them. I know there are behaviors that I do that he does not like, but accepts.

Questions to ask yourself:

1. What can I *not* accept from myself?
2. What behavior can I absolutely *not* accept from my spouse/boyfriend/girlfriend? (Are you accepting this behavior?)
3. What behaviors will I *not* accept from others in my life?

Here are a couple of examples of what I will not accept from myself or from others: For myself, I will not accept giving up. I have found that when I give up on something that I truly believe in, I am basically giving up a piece of myself, which is a self-destructive behavior. From my husband, I will not accept abuse. I will not accept him being physically, sexually, or emotionally abusive towards me. I know this, and he knows this. When we get into arguments—and yes, they get heated—I know and he knows that I will not accept him being abusive and that there will be consequences from this behavior. What I will not accept from others in my life, such as friends and family members, is meanness. I will not accept others, who are supposed to care for and love me, being intentionally mean to me or to anyone else in my life.

Think about what you will not accept from yourself and others, and then decide if the things you cannot accept are happening to you right now. If other people exhibit unacceptable behavior, you need to make a decision on whether these people need to stay in your life. You also need to decide how you can make the necessary changes to stop this unacceptable behavior.

Choices: What a great word and great concept that we are able to have in our lives. Choices—we get to choose every day what we are going to do, what we are going to wear, what we are going to eat, where we are going, who we are going to talk to, or who we want to avoid. If you are a citizen of the United States, you have choices. Do you ever think about this wonderful concept and the fact that you have choices every day on how you are going to live your life? Do you wake up in the morning and ask yourself, "How can I make positive choices in my life today?" Or do you ask yourself, "How can I take responsibility for the choices that I make today?" These usually are not questions that we ask ourselves once a day, once a week, or once a month—for some of us, we never ask these questions. But they are questions that you need to ask yourself regularly, to do what I call a "self-check" on how you are doing in your life. Modern society is fast and self-absorbed, and we, as individuals, are losing touch with ourselves, our loved ones, and others in our community. We have an individual choice to change this in our lives and to make a conscious effort to not allow the chaos in our society to make us feel as if we do not have a choice in our lives. We always have choices. Some will be good, and some will be bad, but we always have a choice.

Whatever choice you make, however, you need to be ready for the consequences. You need to take responsibility for the choice, no matter what the outcome may be.

Question to ask yourself:

1. What is one choice I can make today that will make an improvement in my life? (This choice can be small or large. *Example*: I choose to get up this morning to go to work.)

Choices and *actions* are words that are parallel to one another and should be considered as a thought process. Every day, we make choices for ourselves and act on them. This is called cause and effect. When you open your eyes as you wake, you make the choice of getting up (action), brushing your teeth, taking a shower, washing your face, making coffee, smoking a cigarette, getting ready for work, staying home, making breakfast, taking care of the kids, being bored, watching TV, staying in bed, drinking a beer, eating chocolate, etc. You make these choices every day; you have to make choices. Most of us are not even consciously aware that we make these choices. Most of us have established a routine that does not cause us to think about choices consciously. For me, I get up at the same time every morning and my routine starts on autopilot of letting dog out, making breakfast, jumping in shower; before I know it I am at work. Now don't get me wrong there are some mornings when I don't want to get up and rather stay in bed where I have to think to myself, "Do I want to get up out of this bed and go to work?" I know that doing this action is the right thing to do and I know that if I don't go to work I will not get paid, but I still have to think about it and I still have to make the decision of what I am going to do, I have the choice of staying in bed or getting up and getting ready for work. My point is that from the moment you open your eyes in the morning to the time that you close them to go to sleep, you are making choices, which in turn causes you to act. You need to determine for yourself if the choices you make are good or bad for you. I hope you will look at the choices you make in your life—every moment of every day—take responsibility, and be accountable for these choices and actions.

Questions to ask yourself:

1. Based on the choices I have made today, what actions did I take to make the choice happen?

2. Was this a positive choice, and was the action that occurred positive or negative?
3. What other choice could I have made today that could have had a different outcome?
4. Am I happy with the choices I am making in my life?

Expectations are what we individually perceive as what we want from a person or situation. We all have expectations of others and of situations. Some of these expectations are high, and some are low, but we still expect something. We expect people to behave a certain way, to react a certain way, to treat us in a certain way. We also expect something to happen during certain situations. For example, when I go on vacation, I expect the vacation to be relaxing, fun, stress-free, and filled with activity. I usually take a vacation to get away from my daily life and rejuvenate my psyche. Have you ever gone on a vacation where anything bad that could happen did happen? How did you handle that? I know a time when I did not handle it very well. I became negative and angry and began to have those self-pity thoughts of "why me?" I allowed my vacation to be ruined due to feeling sorry for myself and focusing on the negative issues, instead of focusing on who I was with and that I was away from work and daily life.

I used to have high expectations of everything and everybody, which always made me feel disappointed when *my* expectations did not occur. Expectations can be good or bad. They can cause a person to feel proud or feel disappointed. They can set you up for failure or success. I have been disappointed over and over again due to having high expectations, and this used to get me sad, depressed, and angry. I have realized that my expectations are not the same as someone else's expectations. This does not mean that either of us is right or wrong; we're just different. It is very important for you to know what you expect from yourself, from your spouse, from your children, from your family, from your friends, and from your coworkers, and communicate your expectations to them. My expectations of a relationship may be different from another's expectations. My expectations at work may be different from my coworkers' expectations. My expectations of driving may be different from another driver's. My expectations of my family may be different from other family members' expectations. My expectations of my vacation may be different from what others expect during a vacation.

Be careful not to assume that you know what others expect from you. We are all different, and we all have different expectations. So what do you do if you do have very different expectations from another? Communicate your expectations, be flexible, be able to compromise, and do not set yourself up for failure. That is a *huge* statement, so I'll repeat it: "Do not set yourself up for failure." Again, that goes back to knowing what you want and what you expect for yourself and others. Will you have failures? Absolutely! But the more you know what you want and expect, and the more you prepare for situations, the less disappointed you will be. For example, if I know I have to study for a test, and there is a 50/50 chance that I will pass, I have to expect that I may fail. I have to get in my mind that I may fail and that it will be okay. Of course, I expect (hope) to pass, but I also have to take into account that there is a 50/50 chance that I will fail. You have to have realistic expectations. If you have extremely high expectations, you will set yourself up for failure.

Questions to ask yourself:

1. What do I expect from myself?
2. What do I expect from my spouse/boyfriend/girlfriend?
3. What do I expect from my marriage/relationship?
4. What do I expect from my family members?
5. What do I expect from my coworkers?
6. Are these expectations realistic?
7. Have I communicated my expectations to those in my life?

Personal examples: At work, I have a strong work ethic, but I realize that a lot of people do not. This use to make me angry with my coworkers for not doing their jobs. I would also become frustrated with my bosses for not holding these coworkers accountable for not doing their jobs. I have recognized, however, that even though I have a strong work ethic, I have had to lower my work standard and become more flexible. Now, I have not stopped doing my job—no, no—but I have slowed down my work performance, and I have not stayed late to get work done or gone the "extra mile." I do my job, and I do it very well … but just at a slower pace and with a more realistic standard of what my employer expects from me. I am not adding any extra pressure to myself and not setting myself up for negative thoughts of others, due to my feeling I am working way harder than my peers, again because of my expectation.

Communicating to your spouse or girlfriend/boyfriend what you expect from him or her and the relationship is very important. For example, if you are dating someone, and you expect your relationship to be monogamous, you have to let the other person know that you expect him or her to be faithful in a monogamous relationship. If the other person does not want to be in a monogamous relationship, then you know what he or she expects from this relationship, and you then have the opportunity to decide if you want to be in the relationship. If you are engaged to be married or are in a long-term relationship, have you sat down with the person you are planning to spend the rest of your life with and made a list of what you expect from him or her and from your relationship/marriage?

When I do premarital therapy, I always have the couple write down their expectations of each other and of their marriage. I have them tell each other what they expect, and we discuss these expectations. A lot of times, couples who are getting married for the first time expect a fairy-tale marriage, which does not exist. We discuss this in premarital therapy so that the couple's expectations of each other and of marriage are logical and realistic. This allows the couple to know what each other wants, and they are able to compromise and accept each other better. Discussing expectations may make the couple grow closer together and have a more realistic, loving marriage, but it also may make them realize they are not meant to be together, and they end the relationship before they get married. I have seen it countless times, where marriages were doomed before they actually got married, due to not discussing expectations and being able to compromise with one another. Do not set your marriage up for failure. Marriage and relationships are already hard, don't make them harder.

Children may know what is expected of them, due to getting in trouble after staying out late, writing on the walls, throwing food, not doing their homework, etc. But have you ever sat down with your children and told them what you, as a parent or guardian, expect of them and what will happen if they continue to write on the walls or come home late? By the time children are five or six years old, this is a great way to communicate with them and teach them what is expected of them. It gives them the opportunity to learn about consequences regarding their actions. You tell them that if they continue to not meet your expectations, there will be consequences. You say, "If you continue to come home after dark, I will not allow you to go outside to play after school for a week." If *they* make the decision to stay out after dark, then they know the consequences, which you will have to enforce. Again, this goes back to letting children know what is expected of them, allowing them to make a choice, decide on their action, and then being prepared for the proper consequences, positive or negative. Being able to communicate expectations to those in your life is very important.

Accountability is an action that is similar to responsibility. When you take responsibility for your life, you are accountable for your actions, good or bad. For the most part, people know the difference between right and wrong behaviors. Most of us will try to manipulate or act in a way that is not right, and some of us get away with this behavior sometimes. Now, when I say we get away with this behavior sometimes, that means there will be a time that we do *not* get away with the wrong behavior, and that is when accountability comes into play. When we know consciously that we are doing something that is wrong, and we get caught for this wrong behavior, we need to take responsibility for this action and admit to doing something wrong. How many times have you heard about someone who acted in a way that he or she knew was wrong and was caught? This person may try to explain that he or she did not do this wrong behavior, but if the person does admit to the action, he or she tries to justify why he/she did this behavior and feels that he/she should not be punished. Children as young as two years old learn how to manipulate their parents and "get away" with their wrong behaviors. Adolescents are masters at explaining their actions and justifying why they should not get restrictive or punishment.

Consistency and expectations can help your children to take accountability for their actions. As adults we also try to justify our actions and tell ourselves that we do not have choices—"There was nothing else I could do"—when in a bad situation. I see this behavior every day in the population with which I work. I will see a person smoking methamphetamine, walk up to him, confront him, and he will deny that he is doing any type of illegal drug, even though he knows that I saw him. I have also seen this occur during marital therapy, when one spouse has committed adultery and was caught by the spouse, but and the guilty spouse still tries to explain that he or she did not do it or that it was not his or her "fault."

People must take more responsibility for their actions—evidence is often in black and white, due to modern technology (texting, tweeting, Facebooking, and e-mailing). You need to take responsibility for your actions even when you aren't caught and you need to hold yourself accountable at all times. Being held accountable for your actions and choices in life is the key to a success and fulfilled life.

I guess I need to back up and explain the differences between right, or good, behaviors and wrong, or bad, behaviors. I am aware of cultural and ethical issues within all communities and groups, but I feel that no matter what your ethnicity, there are still behaviors that are wrong or bad. Let me give a couple of examples of behaviors that are never acceptable.

The first one is violence or abuse—physical, emotional, verbal, or sexual abuse to a spouse, companion, family member, friend, stranger, or child. Spouse and intimate-partner abuse or violence is not acceptable, no matter what the other adult has done in the relationship. Adult-on-adult abuse is a sad and shameful act, caused by someone feeling powerless, intimidated, inferior, or fearful. Abuse against a child is the worst abuse a person can commit. I understand that parents or caregivers get upset with their children and make mean and hurtful statements. I also understand that they become so angry and frustrated that they spank or slap their child, but beating, bruising, or assaulting their child is totally different. I do not—and I repeat, *do not*—understand sexual abuse against a child or adult. Sexual abuse is an act that takes thought and planning and should never be committed against anyone, especially children. If you have committed this act or if abuse has occurred to you, I encourage you to please get emotional counseling and support.

The second behavior that is never acceptable is criminal behavior that involves violence, such as murder, rape, robbery with a weapon, terroristic threatening, etc. Yes, I know that people make you mad, and you lose your temper, but that does not give you the right to harm or kill another person. If you are not able to control your emotions, especially anger, please get help with anger-management classes or support groups.

The third unacceptable behavior is substance and alcohol abuse, which consists of doing substances (methamphetamine, cocaine, marijuana, prescription pills, opiates, amphetamines, huffing or sniffing substances) or allowing alcohol to control your life. I do not care if marijuana is legal in some states; it is still a drug that causes mind-altering changes. In my substance-abuse weekly groups, marijuana usage is discussed almost every week. Active drug users continue to complain that they cannot use marijuana. Marijuana is not legal in my home state, and I have to constantly remind the group members that this is an illegal substance. For most of them, marijuana was the first drug they used (or continue to use) that caused them difficulties in their life. If you are abusing alcohol or narcotic substances and are losing control of your life, please seek treatment.

Fourth, infidelity or adultery: this is when one committed partner has a relationship with a person who is not his or her committed partner. This could be an emotional, physical, or sexual relationship. Any relationship that is not with your committed partner and involves intense feelings and actions is wrong. Now, if your committed partner is in agreement to an open relationship, that is different. I am talking about a closed, monogamous relationship, where each party expects the other to be faithful.

Fifth: criminal behaviors, such as theft, fraud, and embezzlement. Yes, I know we all want things that we may not be able to afford, but it does not give you the right to take money or objects that do not belong to you. This refers to taking anything from someone without his or her permission or without paying for the merchandise.

There are other offensive behaviors that are not acceptable: urinating or defecating in public places and sexual encounters in public places. No one wants to see you doing things that should be done in private.

Good, or right, behaviors are much harder and broader to explain. What I may interpret as a good behavior, another may find offensive. For example, the other day, my husband and I were downtown, and a group of kids, eleven to fifteen years old, were playing music on trashcans to get money—and they were really good. My interpretation of this was positive—at least these kids were doing something constructive to make money, instead of selling drugs or living on welfare. My husband, however, felt that they were committing an illegal act—making a bunch of noise and causing a commotion in the streets. We had a disagreement on this topic. Each of us was right, one way or another, but we each felt strongly on the opposite end of the spectrum of what was good or bad behavior.

Most of us view good behavior as behavior that is not offensive, disruptive, criminal, and/or assaultive. Good behavior usually is socially acceptable, kind, pleasant, heartfelt, and polite. Bad behavior is behavior that may hurt someone or cause negative and/or bad feelings or thoughts. This behavior usually has a negative consequence and does not make you feel good about yourself. Behaviors that can be interpreted in different ways, however, should allow room for discussion.

Acceptable behavior is another broad topic. We each have tolerance levels to what we can accept and not accept from others, and I address this in marriage therapy. I explain that acceptable behavior can be different for each person. What may be acceptable to one may be unacceptable to another. I always give an example of a couple who accepted having an open marriage, where they could have sexual relationships with others. I explained that if both partners were accepting of this type of relationship then great, go for it, and have fun. But if one partner is not accepting of this lifestyle but the other is, then this is not good. Both partners have to be in agreement of this behavior and accept that there may be negative consequences from participating in it.

Another example is if partners call each other names and can laugh and joke about the name-calling. If one partner calls the other partner names, and that partner does not like this, then name-calling has to stop, or the marriage/relationship will not survive. Accepting the behavior of the person with whom you have a relationship, intimate or friendly, will determine the outcome of the relationship. Another tricky topic regarding accepting and not accepting other people's behavior is our wonderful family. How do you tell your mother and father that their behavior is not acceptable? Many children, young and old, have had to do this at one time or another. Usually, this does not go over well with the parent, but it is something that you have to decide in order to have a good relationship with your family. If family members' behavior is not "good," and you don't want to accept it, then you have to let them know, and you may have to stop having a relationship with them.

I decided to write this book because of what I have observed from people within my family, my profession, and my community. I am not sure if this realization is due to getting older, wiser, and more aware of people's actions, or if it is the fact that society is more accepting of irresponsible and dysfunctional people. I believe that everyone makes choices in life. Some are good, and some are bad. I have made many bad choices and have behaved in horrible ways. I am not proud of these choices or my behavior. I sometime allow myself to go back to those bad decisions or watch my "mental movie" of myself acting in an unflattering way. I then realize that I had to make those choices and act that way to be the person I am today. Even though you make bad choices or act in "bad" ways, you can learn from these bad choices and make a conscious effort to not make the same choice. "Live and learn" is my motto. Live your life, make choices, accept these choices, learn from your choices, and move on with your life. Moving on is very important. If you do not move on with your life and learn from your mistakes, your life will move on without you leaving you wondering, wondering, wondering, how your life has passed you by and why you continue to be bored and unhappy.

Chapter 2

· · · · · · · · · · · · · · · · · ·

Boredom, Depression, or Midlife Crisis

· · · · · · · · · · · · · · · · · ·

Nobody is bored when he is trying to make something that is beautiful, or to discover something that is true.
—William Inge

A lot of people seem to describe themselves as "depressed," but what does depression really mean? Depression is defined as a mental disorder, characterized by episodes of all-encompassing low mood, accompanied by low self-esteem and loss of interest or pleasure in normally enjoyable activities. Major depressive disorder is a disabling condition that adversely affects a person's family, work, or school life, sleeping and eating habits, and general health. Depression is a serious mental-health disorder and needs to be assessed and treated. The symptoms of depression and being bored, however, are very similar. It is unclear if boredom causes depression or if depression causes boredom. The main 2 questions on a depression assessment are, have you lost interest in all activities and do you no longer find pleasure in activities? These are good questions for both depression and boredom. Of course, if you are depressed, you will not want to do the activities due to not having the motivation to do it, due to not having the energy to do it or due to not caring enough to want to do it. But if you are bored, you still may not want to do the activities, but this may be due to you no longer have interest in that activity, or you may have mastered the activity and found that it does not stimulate you anymore. You may realize it is not your "thing," or you just don't want to do it again. This does not mean you are depressed, you just may be bored with the activity and you need to do something new. Again, depression and boredom can look the same, but if you really ask yourself the tough questions you may be able to recognize the difference.

For example, I play golf with my husband a couple of times a month. I like being outside and spending time with my husband, but after the ninth or tenth hole, I start to want to do something else. I really don't want to focus on hitting a golf ball anymore. I have lost interest in this activity. After nine or ten holes, I am ready to move on to something new. Golf bores me after a couple of hours. Am I depressed because I don't want to play golf every day? No. It just is not my thing! Now, if my husband, who absolutely loves golf, does not want to play golf every day, there may be some concern regarding depression.

Take me to a zoo, and I can be there all day, watching the animals and talking to others about the animals. I find myself smiling, happy, and content. This is my thing! If my husband asked me to go to the zoo, I would have to be deathly sick to not go. Just because you do not enjoy something, does not mean you are depressed. With depression, you will experience several other symptoms, such as fatigue, crying, irritability, thoughts and feelings of worthlessness, inappropriate guilt or regret, helplessness, hopelessness, and self-hatred. With boredom, you may also feel these same symptoms but for different reasons. With depression and boredom, you really have to ask yourself why you are having these symptoms and what is going on in your life that is making you unhappy.

Everyone goes through periods of depression, which I call "situational depression." When you look at the symptoms of depression, they are very similar to being bored, but there is a difference. Being bored is a state of mind that you can change by making different choices and following through with those choices. Depression is a chemical imbalance that occurs due to many reasons. As mentioned above, anyone may experience short-term depression ("situational depression"), but longer term may be a major depressive disorder, which can be helped with antidepressants, therapy, and change in lifestyle.

Situational depression usually occurs after a death, divorce, childbirth, loss of a job, or other life-changing experience. This depression usually lasts for one to three months. In my opinion, everyone—yes, everyone—experiences situational depression at least once in their lifetime. There is no way you can experience a loss and not feel sad, fatigued, hopeless, or unmotivated. You will have to go through the stages of grief: denial, anger, bargaining, depression, and acceptance. It is a process, and you will get through it. Now, if this process takes longer than three months, I encourage you to see a mental-health professional for help with depression.

Now, I would like you to do a self-assessment by asking the following questions:

Do I spend a lot of time by myself?
Am I lonely?
Do I want to be by myself? If not, what can I do to meet people?
What is stopping me from interacting with others or meeting someone new?
What would my life look like if I was happy?
Why can't it look like that?
What is stopping me from being happy?

Answer truthfully, and write out the answers. Then write out a plan for how you can do more of the activities you mention. Attempt to make changes in your thoughts and actions, based on how you answered these questions. This exercise will take time. If you truly apply yourself to making changes, based on these questions, and you begin to feel better about yourself and your life, then you probably are more bored than depressed. But you will have to make changes. Change in your life will not happen if you continue to sit there and not do anything. You have to make it happen.

With this exercise, you will have to actually do the things you wrote down that you want to do. You may not want to proceed with this exercise until after you finish this book, but I do want you to recognize what you want to change and identify how this can be done.

After completing this book and truly applying what you want to change, if you still feel absolutely bored, with ongoing negative thoughts of self, then you will need to seek more therapeutic care. There may be more going on with you than boredom.

Like many of you, I have gone through situational depression several times, but each time, I recognized the symptoms and was able to get through it. It took me several weeks to go through the process, but after I did, I felt like myself again. That does not mean I did not have moments of sadness afterward, but not to the extent that I had when I was going through the process. Whenever I felt the sadness, anger, or blah feelings, I would do a self-assessment, asking myself the above questions, and determine if I was depressed or bored. Most of the time, it was boredom. Once I was able to wrap my mind around being bored and made decisions on making changes in my life, these depressive symptoms and the feeling of boredom subsided.

Each time I found myself bored, I realized I did not have any new goals or plans. I was going through life day to day, with nothing to keep the passion alive or give me purpose, everyone needs to have a sense of purpose in their life. A couple of years ago I realized that I had not established any new goals for myself since 2000. I did not have a purpose in my life. Goals and having a purpose (small or large) are very important to your mental state. Think about it; if you do not have goals or you do not feel you have a purpose in life, then what is the point of getting up in the morning? You start asking yourself, "Why am I here? What am

I suppose to do with my life? Who cares about me?" Please think about this for a minute.

Think about the goals you have right now for yourself.
Think about the reason you exist right now.
What is your purpose, and how fulfilling is this purpose?

In my twenties and thirties, I wanted to have children, and my goal was always to be a mother. That was my focus for a good ten years. I thought that being a mother was my purpose, but due to circumstances beyond my control, I did not have children. When I turned thirty, I did not know who I was or who I was going to be, because I was not a mother. I had suicidal thoughts because I didn't know what I was going to do with my life. I hated everyone who was pregnant or who had children and resented my friends, family, and God. In my twenties, I completed my bachelor's degree in psychology and even started work on my master's degree, but I did this for all the wrong reasons and never considered myself a career woman. I was going to be a mother, damn it! After turning thirty and divorcing my first husband, I needed to change my goals and focus on something over which I had control—before I went crazy. So in 2000, I set the goal of completing my master's degree in social work and completing my hours to accomplish my goal of becoming a Licensed Clinical Social Worker (LCSW) by the time I turned thirty-five years old.

By the time I turned thirty-five, I had completed all the schooling that I wanted to complete, and I had my LCSW. During this time, I remarried and focused on this new marriage. I still did not have any children, even though we tried. Now, I am forty years old, and I feel that I am too old to have children. Thankfully, I have come to terms with not having children, and I still have a fulfilled life. I did not accomplish my goal—my dream—of being a mother, which at first was hard to accept, but I came to the realization that I needed to let go of this dream. After that, boredom crept into my life again, and those negative thoughts and feelings of anger, sadness, depression, and hopelessness crept into my life—again. I started to ask myself questions, such as "What am I going to do now? What do I have to look forward to doing? What is my purpose in this world?" I felt lost and confused. So, *again*, I had to do my self-assessment and honestly ask myself, "Do I want to let this dream that did not come true ruin my life and make me miserable for the rest of my life? Or do I want to move forward, make a new life for myself, and be happy with all the good things that I have?" We always focus on what we do not have, instead of what we do have. Well, again this got me thinking—should I go back to school? (No—hell no, don't want to do that.) Should I become a realtor? (Maybe—we'll see.) Should I plan another trip? (Of course!) But I could only plan so many trips, so I evaluated myself *again*, and that is how this book got started.

So my goal was to start writing a book. More and more, it sounds like I was going through a midlife crisis, but this allowed me to focus on a goal that I have always wanted to fulfill. I realized that we should always have goals that we want to fulfill, no matter how old we get. I know that once I fulfill this goal, I will have to focus on a new goal, and then another new goal to always feel encouraged and motivated in life. I think that is the biggest issue people have when they get older—they do not have goals anymore. They lose their zest for life and stop moving forward. They become stale and stall in life. The worst decision my mom made in her life was to retire at sixty years old. Since she retired, she has been diagnosed with Alzheimer's disease and has given up on life. Her statement at retirement was, "I don't have to do anything, because I am retired," and basically, she did nothing. In my opinion, her mind got weak, and she got bored, and now she is in a nursing facility. Now, I know many would disagree with me, but this is my opinion of my mother's prognosis. It scares me to death to know that I possibly could develop Alzheimer's, and I have been making a conscious effort to keep my mind and body busy and active, to not allow myself to get bored and complacent.

I am not saying that this is easy and that you have to "snap out of" being bored, because if it were that easy, then I would not be writing this book.

You can consciously decide, however, what you want in your life and then go for it. It won't be easy, but it can be done. Goals and purpose will help you make changes—even baby-step changes—toward a better, healthier you. The questions I want you to ask yourself regarding your goals are:

What would I like to accomplish in the next six months?
What would I like to accomplish in the next year?
What would I like to accomplish in the next three years?
What is stopping me from accomplishing these goals?
Who is holding me back from accomplishing these goals?
What are my fears regarding accomplishing my goal?

Think about your goals, and then write them down. I want you to be honest and realistic with the goals that you want to accomplish. For example, when I made the goal at age thirty of getting my LCSW by the age of thirty-five, I could have set the goal of completing it by the time I turned thirty-three years old. I knew, however, that giving myself three years to accomplish a goal that I knew would take longer would have set me up for failure. I would not accomplish this goal in three years—I did not want to stop living my life to go to school and complete clinical hours. I knew I needed to have fun and live too, so setting my goal five years out gave me time to enjoy life while still focusing on a goal. If I completed my goal early, that would be a bonus, but as it turned out, in those five years I completed my master's degree, got a divorce, moved, got remarried, and moved again. I received my LCSW six months after I turned thirty-five—goal accomplished!

So again, when you answer the above questions, please be truthful with yourself and acknowledge what will and will not help you accomplish your goal. I also want you to acknowledge what fears you may have when you accomplish the goal. For example, if you want to lose a hundred pounds, you need to set a realistic time frame and a realistic diet and exercise plan. You also have to acknowledge that when you lose a hundred pounds, you will be a different person, and your life will change. You may fear that if you lose the weight, you will be expected to get a better job, have children, or dress sexier. This might sound exciting and good, but many people fear change and the unknown, and that may sabotage their goals. You also have to take into consideration that those around you may have fears about you accomplishing your goals and may try to sabotage you accomplishing the goal. For example, husband or wife may fear that if the spouse loses weight, he or she will leave the marriage or if you complete your college degree you may not want to stay home with the children. These are just examples, but I want you to think deeply about how your goals will make an impact on your life and those around you. Be honest and truthful with yourself when you make your goals and look at the *whole* picture of how your goals will give you purpose and fulfillment.

How does boredom affect adults? Boredom can have a big impact on our life patterns and can jeopardize our relationships, our careers, our health, and our sanity. It can have long-lasting effects that cannot be erased or easily fixed.

I asked people from all ages, ethnicities, and social classes about being bored. Many reported that they do not have time to be bored, but still had a feeling of being unfulfilled. This got me thinking again, is it boredom or just not being fulfilled? These concepts would go hand in hand. If you are not feeling fulfilled in your life, more than likely you are not happy, which can cause you to feel empty, sad, bored and hopeless. So is it boredom, depression, unhappiness, or midlife crisis? If we could wake up one morning and pinpoint which one it was, there would be no need for therapists.

Boredom can come at any age and during any time of life. I am busy with my life, but I still have times when I am bored, which is never good for me, emotionally or physically. When I turned forty and questioned my goals and had negative feelings regarding my life and my purpose, I wondered whether I was going through a midlife crisis. I asked friends who were forty or who were about to turn forty how they felt about their lives and what they enjoyed doing. Most of my friends have children, but their children are older and more independent. They explained that their children keep them busy due to their schedules, but they acknowledged that they still feel like something is missing in their lives. Like me, most of them stated they did not know what they want from life and explained they were "bored." The joke became, "What do I want to do when I grow up?" They too are feeling bored and unsure about their lives. I asked them, "Bored with what?" Their response usually was, "With life." They are bored with their spouse, job, sex, time with friends, activities—just bored. One of my friends stated, "I am bored with going out to eat and having a couple of drinks. It is the same ol' same ol', so I'd rather just stay home and watch *Housewives*." I had to laugh, because I could relate to her.

So again, is this boredom, depression, or a midlife crisis? At times, I feel it is all three, although if it is depression, there are a lot of people who are depressed. I am not convinced that all these people are depressed; they are just not fulfilled, for whatever reason. I have to laugh every time I see a medical provider, and he or she asks, "Are you feeling hopeless about your life? Or have you lost pleasure in activities?" I want to scream, *yes, yes, yes*! I know I am not depressed, just bored. It is never good when I get bored. I start spending money, having irrational thoughts, and crave something "wild," like sky diving, riding a bull, having an orgy—whatever will stimulate my mind and/or body. I'm not saying doing these things are wrong and should not be done, but when I am bored, I have an overwhelming yearning that takes over and makes me crave something—*something*. It is funny, because when I tell my family and friends I am getting bored, they know that this is not good for me. My husband will ask, "Do I need to be worried?" My sister just shakes her head and smiles, knowing, "Oh-oh, this is not good." I am not bipolar or manic, I have never been diagnosed with a mental illness; in fact, I am the person who diagnoses others with mental illness. So I don't want you to think that there is something mentally wrong with me—not entirely. I realize that I may be the average middle-aged woman who is willing to admit that she is bored and needs to do something fun and exciting! I need to have goals and purpose! I need to feel happy!

Could I be going through a midlife crisis? It is starting to look more and more like this is a good possibility. Let's see … I am forty-one years old; I have a successful career, a good marriage, no children; and I am stable, wishing I had done more in my life, thinking about what I would change in my life, regretting some choices I have made in the past, thinking about what I want to do with the rest of life—yup, it sounds like a midlife crisis. Right now, all I want to do is something fun and exciting. What does this mean? I am not sure anymore. Yes, I have jumped out of a plane and ridden a mechanical bull, but I have never been in an orgy or cheated on my husband—but I do have those thoughts (sad but true). Will I follow through with these thoughts? Doubt it, but it is still an unsettling feeling when these thoughts come to me. At times, I wonder what makes me not act on my thoughts, and then I remember those wonderful morals, values, and feelings of shame if I were to do something out of my comfort zone, which again makes me wonder, "Is that my problem? Am I worried about doing something that will make me feel uncomfortable? Am I holding back on doing things that I really want to do because I am afraid that people will look at me with *judgment*? Ouch! I always say that I am envious of the people who can be free in what they say or do, and they don't care what others think. I am drawn to these types of people, but I am unable to act on what I really want to do. Maybe turning forty years old has made me realize that I need to be free and say "fuck it" and do what I want to do. Several of my friends who are forty or turning forty have discussed being more vocal about our feelings and needs. We are more vocal about people who "piss us off," and we let them know when they do.

It is really a liberating feeling to speak my mind and not care what people think, but then again, the morals and values seep back in, and I backtrack and feel "bad." I hate feeling "bad" or hurting other people. As a social worker, I am the person who is supposed to make everyone feel good, not bad. I think this is another reason I get bored. I see people do what they want and have no cares in the world. They do drugs, are homeless, do not work, do not pay taxes, live off other people, beat their spouses and children, have sex with multiple partners, and most of the time, they do not feel bad about this—unless they get caught. Basically, they are not taking responsibility for their actions, but they manage to live through life and at times appear happier and more content with life, but are they really content and happy?

Now, I am not saying I want to become a drug-addicted, antisocial, husband-beating woman, but there are times when I see these people get away with their bad behaviors, and they don't seem to be bored. They do appear angry, confused, narcissistic, weak, unhappy, manipulating, co-dependent and just down right miserable. In my experience, these individuals report feeling bored and not having anything to do. They are not willing to accept consequences and are unable to understand that they can make changes in their life. They appear to have no direction, therefore leading them to behave in ways that are not healthy and productive. Let's look at what boredom means again,

Boredom is an emotional state, experienced when an individual is left without anything in particular to do and is not interested in his or her surroundings. I have plenty to do, but it all bores me. I can name at least ten things I can do in a day, but none of them seems fun or exciting. Therefore, I categorize them as boring, which makes me bored. You can see where this is a fine line. What a mess! So what is a girl to do about this boredom thing? Get a hobby—sure, I can do that, but again, what? My husband always tells me I need a hobby. I agree with him, but I'm not sure what my hobby will be—golf, tennis, knitting, yoga, running? I can and have done all these things, but I'm still bored. Do I have ADD (attention deficit disorder)? I know adult ADD is becoming the "new" diagnosis, and there may be some advantages to getting tested for this, but do I want to take medication? No! Do I want to teach myself how to entertain myself and not be bored? Yes! And there it goes again—teaching myself how not to be bored. Making myself look at my life and make changes so that I can be happier and fulfilled. Hoping that by making small changes, such as acknowledging my boredom, setting new goals, and focusing on people and things that make me happy, maybe I can stop being *bored*! Maybe I can feel better about myself and feel happier and fulfilled!

I cannot believe I am fortysomething. I don't want to act forty years old. I don't want to act old and stuffy, since that is what "old" people do. I want to act young and carefree. They say being forty is the new thirty. Maybe this is my problem; I have not allowed reality to set in that I am officially getting old. Maybe that is why I am bored all the time—I am trying to figure out where I fit in. I want to act young and wild, but I don't want to look like "that person" who is forty and acts like she is twenty. There I go again with my morals and values of not wanting to look "bad." I don't want to be a "cougar," but I do have thoughts about being with a younger man who is buffed up, hot, and fertile. My husband's favorite line is that he is going to trade me in for two twenty-year-olds, but I know he won't—or will he? He can't hang with me, so I wonder how he would do with two twenty-year-olds. Now me, on the other hand … hm-m-m, I wonder. Again, there goes those thoughts that I should not act on—damn it!

Turning forty has its advantages, so they say. People say at forty, you are more secure with yourself, you are smarter about the world, and you have a career and are more financially stable. For those who have children, most of your children are older and more independent, and you have more free time. (For those who are having children at forty, are you crazy? I can't even imagine, but that is just me.) At forty, you are at the prime of your life. Then why am I bored? This is the prime of my life? Really? Let's see … I work all day; exercise to lose no weight; come home; cook a boring dinner or go out to dinner for the same food; lie on my couch; and go to bed, just to do it all again the next day. I try to throw in a couple of vacations a year to spice things up, but they only last for a week or two. I know this sounds like "poor me," and it is my fault that I am not doing more in my life. Again, I am bored, and don't know what to do. Oh yeah, let me go look on my Facebook page again! Turning forty has some advantages. Like I said earlier, you can express yourself more and not look stupid or righteous but look sophisticated and intelligent, because remember, you have life experiences. You are able to not give a shit what other people think—really, not sure if I have mastered that one.

Due to all these conflicting feelings and thoughts I started to re-evaluate myself and my life. Yes, I am more financially secure, and I have to admit… Sometimes I am thankful for not having children when I hear and see what my friends who do have children are going through. The biggest struggle I have had with getting older is taking care of my mother, who I've mentioned was diagnosed with Alzheimer's at sixty-three years old. Several of my friends also are taking care of their parents due to failing health. This has been a whole other reality check that life is not as fun as I thought it would be. It has been a real wake-up call for me. My mother is now seventy years old and lives in an assisted living facility—my siblings and I no longer are able to take care of her. It has been very eye opening and sad to see my mom not remember her life. It is sad to see that at the end of her life she cannot remember the ones who love her and is in a facility with strangers. It makes me wonder if this is what I have to look forward to. It has made me think about death and mortality, which I have not done before. The realization that life is short and precious. Now, if you ask my mom if she had a good life, she will tell you she has and that she is thankful for all that she has experienced, even though she can't remember what she has experienced. She somehow has a sense of being satisfied with her life, and it comforts me to know that she feels that way. Since she was diagnosed, I have had this feeling that I need to do everything I want to do quickly, before I too lose my mind. My fear that I will also develop Alzheimer's may be playing a part in my ongoing thoughts of wanting to do something "wild" before I can't remember how to be wild. When I went through all my mom's belongings when she moved to the facility, I realized she only had a couple of things that were of real value, most of the stuff she had was "junk". Throughout her years she had bought and inherited items that did not have any purpose or meaning. I realized that we surround ourselves with "junk" that usually distracts us or clutters our lives, causing us to focus on aspects in our life that do not really matter. For example, clothes, oh my God, my mom had so many clothes, piles of clothes, some she never wore, some she could not fit into anymore, clothes and shoes everywhere, even though she usually wore the same outfits over and over again. As a society, we have become a materialistic world. We buy way to many "things" with the hope that these "things" will make us feel better about ourselves, but do they? I have found that most often we buy "things" to replace a void in our lives, which helps distract us from what we really need to deal with. After cleaning out my mother's "junk" I decided to start getting rid of my junk and clutter. I stopped focusing on material objects that I thought made me feel better about myself and started to focus on my inner self and those around me that I love. Now I am not saying I don't buy me clothes, shoes, jewelry and "things" but I am much more mindful of buying "things" because I need it or truly want it. When I go shopping I ask myself, "Do I really need this or want it, or will it just become junk?"

What "junk" do you have that you want to get rid of?
Why are you holding on to this "junk"?

I have realized that life is too short, and you need to live it while you can. Being bored and waiting for life to take control is not the way to go. You have to take control of your life. Whatever age you are, you are still alive, and you are still able to make good decisions about what you want for the rest of your life. The rest of your life may be a day or it may be fifty years. *You* still have choices. You still have time to exercise, start a new hobby or activity, make a new friend, or start a new relationship. You still have time to accomplish the goals that you want to accomplish. You still have time to love, hug, kiss, and say thank you and I am sorry to the people you love and who love you. I sometimes feel that as people get older, they think they can't do the things they could do when they were younger. This may be true physically, but you still can do most activities; it may take a little longer and may be more of a challenge, but you still can do it. It does not matter how old or young you are. You still have time to not be bored with your life and live a life that is active and fulfilled.

As I have hit middle age, I have found that at times, getting with my girlfriends even gets boring. I get bored with the same conversations about children, gossiping about others, husband troubles, and work issues. I have realized that when you get a bunch of middle-aged women together, the conversation always goes to someone complaining. I don't want to hear complaining; I want to have fun! Again, have fun! So it makes me ask the question, are we bored and unhappy and therefore we complain about our lives and about others for entertainment? Do we feel we have to complain to have something in common? Is this what getting older is all about—little old ladies complaining about their lives? I have to admit that there are times when I think about the should have, could have, and would haves, and I have found that it is not healthy. What I have found helpful is to identify the should have, could have, and would haves and see which ones I can still accomplish and acknowledge those that I can't. This allows me to focus on things that I still want to do and to stop dwelling on the things that I can't do. A good example would be my not having a child. If I allow myself to focus on all the reasons I did not have a child, I would become an angry, depressed, and resentful midlife women. I would continue to blame other people for the choices I made that did not allow me to have a child. I would be angry with and resentful of all my friends who had children, and I would basically start to hate children. Wow, that sounds horrible. I would become depressed, and it would be a constant dark place for me. But by acknowledging that it did not happen, it will not happen, and that it is okay it did not happen, I have been able to focus on what my life is going to look like, child-free, and what I want to do with my life instead of dwelling on what I was not able to do. I have been able to "let it go" and move on. Do I still have days when I wish I had a child? Yes, but there are only a couple of days a year, instead of every day or every month when my monthly friend comes to visit.

You have to move forward before life leaves you. I recommend that you re-evaluate your should have, could have, and would haves every five years and make a decision of what you can still accomplish. Then let go of the things that you can't change or do anymore. I always tell people that as humans, we evolve and change every eight to ten years. We are never the same person we were ten years ago. We grow and mature;

therefore, we change. I am not saying we change who we are, but we change what we want, how we view the world and others, what we want to do, and hopefully, what we want to achieve. I am definitely not the same person I was when I was twenty years old, which is a good thing, I am still me—just older, wiser, more confident, a little jaded, and a lot less naive.

So I want you to ask yourself the following questions and be honest with yourself. Really think about your regrets, and ask yourself if you can still do any of the could have, would have, and should haves that you continue to think about and that cause you sadness and regret. Can you make them right, or can you accept that they are not going to happen and let them go?

- Are you happy with the choices you have made in your life?
- What do you regret the most about your life?
- If you could change one thing in your life, what would it be?
- Could you make the change now?
- If you cannot make the change, can you let it go and not dwell on it anymore?
- Can you accept the choices you have made and live with them?

Get older is not easy, and sometimes it's hard to accept, but aging is a fact of life, and it will happen no matter what, so accept it. Embrace it, and take advantage of all the experiences, lessons, and memories that you have from your past. I always say, never forget your past, but forgive those who may have hurt you or caused you pain. If you continue to focus on your should have, could have, and would haves, you will be unhappy, depressed, and bored, and you will go through a midlife crisis that may cause you more grief and heartache. Again, be careful with thinking about the would have, could have, and should haves, and embrace what you can change—and let go of what you can't.

I feel I have done more in the past seven years than in my whole life, but at times, I still feel empty. I lived in Hawaii for six years, but by the fourth year, I was bored and ready to get off the island. I would go scuba diving and count the fish that I had already seen a hundred times, instead of enjoying the beauty of the fish. What was wrong with me? My husband accused me of never being satisfied, which got me thinking, What would make me feel satisfied? At times, I feel life is passing me by, and if I don't jump on the train, then I will never get on. I think this is pretty much a midlife statement. In the past, I had a hard time being mindful of what I am doing and experiencing. About three years ago, I completed a training on being mindful and found that I was not comfortable with being mindful of my surroundings and of my thoughts. It was not something I had done in the past, which is why I never felt content with all the experiences I have had. Sometimes I find myself looking at pictures of myself doing something great, and I feel like I was not there. I was not being mindful of the moment or the experience.

Being mindful is when you are able to be in the moment and take in the experience, feeling, and emotion that you are having at the moment. I look back at my life, and I have done a lot of things, but I have not been in the moment to actually feel the experience. I have found that when I do something new, it is like I am checking it off a list and not actually living in the moment and being grateful for what I am doing. Being mindful of yourself and experiences is very important. Over the past couple of years, I have trained my mind to take a moment and make a conscious effort to be in the moment. Now I do this all the time. When I spend time with my friends and laugh and enjoy myself, when my husband gives me a hug and I feel his body against mine, when I see a play and recognize the emotions I am having, when I go on a hike and breathe the fresh air, when I am at work and recognize I am actually helping a person—I am mindful of all these wonderful experiences that in the past, I missed.

Being mindful is something that I want you to start doing. It only takes a second to take a long breathe, look around, and make a mental note of where you are, what you are doing, who you are with, and how you are feeling. If you are able to be in the moment, then you are able to recognize all the positives you have in your life, instead of focusing on all the negatives. A smile, a hug, or a thank-you can make a difference in your life. Now, if you recognize all the negatives in your life and feel that there are no positives, you have to make a decision to make changes. You have to become mindful of the changes you want to make, and then make a plan of how you are going to make the changes. Being mindful of the good and bad in your life can make a difference in how you want to see your future and what you want to experience. As you read this book, you have to be mindful of what you are feeling, and acknowledge what you are thinking. You have to be in the moment and be truthful with yourself. When you are depressed, it is difficult to be in the moment. You usually just feel blah and numb; you really don't feel anything but sadness. With boredom, you can feel the moment and actually make a point of getting up and making change. If you find yourself focusing on your past, the could have, would have and should have's you need to make a conscious effort of focusing on your future and making changes based on what you have learned from the past.

My suggestion is for you to do some soul-searching and figure out what is going on in your brain and your life. This may take a while to do, but you really have to be honest with yourself when trying to decide what you are going through. You will not be happy until you can determine what will make you happy. So answer a couple of questions that may help you through this process. I want you to think about the answers, but I also want you not to overthink them. Write down the first answer that comes to mind.

- Am I happy?
- If I am not happy, what makes me unhappy?
- When do I feel happy?
- What makes me smile?
- What activities make me feel content and fulfilled?
- When was the last time I did this activity?
- If it has been a long time since doing this activity, why?

I am bored and I am TIRED of it!!

- Am I bored?
- When was the last time I did not feel bored?
- Do I feel fulfilled by my daily life schedule?
- Do I need some time just for me?
- At what age was I the happiest? Why?
- What do I want to accomplish in my life?
- Have I accomplished my goals?

Chapter 3

Boredom and Eating, Relationships, Children, and Addiction

> *Life is never boring, but some people choose to be bored. The concept of boredom entails an inability to use up present moments in a personally fulfilling way. Boredom is a choice; something you visit upon yourself, and it is another of those self-defeating items that you can eliminate from your life.*
> —Wayne W. Dyer

Boredom affects every aspect of your life. In this chapter I will discuss how boredom affects you, your loved ones, and your health. Boredom has a ripple effect on how you live your life. You have the choice to change this to a positive ripple instead of a massive tidal wave.

Boredom and Eating

Have you ever wondered how a person can become obese? Maybe this is something that you are struggling with and are tired of feeling miserable about your weight and health. I am not obese, but I am overweight, and I struggle every day—yes, every day—with what I should eat and with what I want to eat. I eat when I am not hungry, and I overeat when I am starving. I try to exercise every day, but this is also a struggle. I can find a zillion reasons why I cannot exercise every day, when in actuality, there is nothing more important than my health and the way I feel about myself. I always feel better after I exercise, even when I'm sore, so why don't I do it every day?

Obesity is due to inactivity and overeating. What do you do when you are bored? I like to eat and do absolutely nothing. Eating and boredom go hand in hand. When you are bored and you walk into the kitchen, what do you do? Open up a cabinet or refrigerator and see what looks appetizing. You don't care if it is healthy; you want to eat something to pass the time—usually something gooey and yummy.

You may think if you eat this candy bar, it will satisfy a want or need or just time, but ten minutes later, you are in the kitchen again. You are not hungry; you are bored. You are trying to find something to occupy that emptiness—not the emptiness in your stomach but the emptiness in your life. When you find yourself standing in front of the refrigerator, you need to ask yourself, "Am I hungry or bored?" If you are hungry, eat something fulfilling, not junk. If you are bored, walk outside, find something to distract your mind, and do something other than eat. Most obese people will tell you that they eat out of boredom, not hunger. Obesity is an epidemic in our society. Children who used to go out and play now sit in front of a computer or video game and eat. Again, they are not eating because they are hungry; they are eating because they are bored and preoccupied with playing on the computer. Kids, like adults, eat to fulfill something that they are lacking.

I know this feeling. I eat when I am bored, especially chocolate. I love chocolate! The twenty pounds I need to lose are due to boredom. Weight issues only get worse as you get older; it is harder to lose those extra pounds. You have to be careful with what you eat, and you have to stay active! If someone says, "I am active and can't lose weight," then it has to be what that person is eating. Be honest with yourself, and admit to all the chocolate you are eating. It always amazes me that I can justify my chocolate addiction, but at the end of the day, when I get on a scale, I feel bad about myself. I have the LIVESTRONG and LOSE IT! application on my phone. I will put in my daily calories—or the calories to which I want to admit—and it looks good. I am below my daily calories allowance, but I have not lost any weight. Why? I have had to teach myself to be honest with putting in every piece of food that I have eaten that day. Since being honest, I have lost some weight; honesty is the key. Being active and not eating when you are bored are also very important when trying to lose weight.

Relationships

Boredom in a relationship is a common experience, but boredom can be devastating to your relationship, especially your intimate relationships. As humans, we have a need to be connected with others. We have a need to feel loved and give love. We have to be desired, and we have to be sexual. Relationships make us happy, but they also make us miserable. I have asked myself many times, why do people get married? Why do we put ourselves through the ups and downs of being in a marriage or relationship? Why do we get out of one miserable relationship to jump right back into another relationship? Well, since I have been married and divorced and remarried, I have come to the conclusion that I am happier being married than when I was divorced and single. Yes, I liked the freedom of being single and doing whatever I wanted to do, but at the end of the day, I did not have anyone who was consistently there for me, to care for me and love me. So I remarried and again asked myself, why did I get married? I can honestly say that even though we have our ups and downs, I'd rather be married than single. I know my husband loves me, and I love him, even when he gets on my last nerve. I know he will be there for me if I need him. Now, do I get bored in this marriage? Absolutely! Do I look at him at times and think, why am I with him? Absolutely. But then reality sets in, and I am thankful for him and the relationship we have. This does not make my marriage any easier, but I know that we have to work at our issues and not become complacent in our relationship.

As a marriage therapist, I see that the biggest complaint that couples have is that they are bored with one another. They usually do not come straight out and say this, but they definitely imply it. They usually complain that they have nothing in common and do not like doing activities together. Their sex life is boring and dull, and they don't find each other attractive. There is no spark! There have been a thousand books on how to spark your love life. In any grocery or convenience store, you can find *Cosmo* or *Glamour* with advice on how to charge up your love life. Still, thousands of divorces occur every year.

My first marriage got boring after about six years. Our once very active sex life got dull and boring, and we stopped having passionate, need-you-now sex. My ex-husband started to cheat, and a divorce occurred. Now, in my second marriage, we are approaching seven years of marriage, and those nagging thoughts of being bored are creeping into my mind. I don't want my marriage to end, but I have to ask myself, why am I getting bored? Is it the seven-year itch? If you have been married for over seven years, can you relate to the seven-year itch? With both of my husbands, the start of the relationship was wonderful—great conversation, had a lot in common, great sex—but then it started to dwindle. Is this normal, or does it have something to do with me? There has to be something wrong with me, right? Again, I asked my friends and peers about this, and couples come to see me, and it clarifies that there is nothing wrong with me, but there is something going on that causes couples to feel this way, time after time. You see, divorce rates at over 50 percent—but why?

My opinion is that when you meet someone, it is new and exciting. You have wonderful conversations as you get to know each other. You do new activities with one another, and you are willing to try new activities to please your new partner. And of course, you are having great, exciting, passionate sex. The relationship is new and wonderful—who has time to think about being bored? However, as the relationship moves forward, you have talked about everything you can think of, you have tried all the activities together—some you like; some you do not—you have tried every sex position you can think of, you start to have children, your working life takes over ... and guess what? That relationship is usually put to the side, and you stop having fun. *You have to continue to have fun!* I know this, and I try very hard to keep my relationship fun, but I have to admit, it is hard. How do you keep a relationship healthy, fun, exciting, and happy? First, answer the following questions and again, be truly honest with yourself:

- How long have you been in this relationship?
- Why do you stay in this relationship?
- What do you get out of being in this relationship?
- What makes you happy in this relationship?
- What do you find attractive about your mate?
- Are you *in love* with your spouse—not just love and care for your partner, but *in* love?
- Do you respect your partner?
- Do you trust you partner?
- How often do you have sex?
- You may have sex often, but how often is it the "good" sex?
- How committed are you to this relationship? (Do you have any thoughts about leaving the relationship?)
- When was the last time you went on a date?
- When was the last time you did something that made your partner smile?
- When was the last time your partner did something that made you smile?
- What is the one thing that you cannot accept about your partner?
- Are you able to tell your partner that you cannot accept this?
- Do you feel this relationship is safe?
- Can you talk to your partner about your concerns, and will he/she listen to you?

You have to be truthful when you answer these questions so that you can determine what will make you happy in this relationship and to determine if this relationship is healthy and good for you. Relationships are hard, and they are usually the biggest reason why we are happy, sad, angry, or depressed. Think about it: when you are happy in your relationship, how do you feel? Usually, the answer is wonderful, happy, fulfilled, elated! But when you are not happy in a relationship, you most likely feel sad, angry, bored, and miserable. We should not rely on our partners to make us happy, but they do have a significant impact on our lives and our happiness. I always say that you have to make yourself happy first, and then you should make your relationship happy, and then make others happy. The sequence of happiness should be you, partner, and then children. Many will disagree with this concept and feel that children should be first, but think about it—if you are not happy with yourself, and you're not in a happy and healthy relationship, then how can you be a healthy parent? Your unhappiness will ooze out to your children, one way or another. You and your partner have to be happy together by going on date nights and spending time together, and then this love and happiness will be shown to your children. I am not saying that you have to spend all of your time making yourself happy and ignore your partner and children, or that you have to spend all of your time making your partner happy and ignore your children. You do have to balance all of these so you can be the best self, partner, and parent. So the question is, how do you make yourself happy and avoid these nagging feelings of being bored?

First, you have to be honest with yourself regarding your relationship. After making the determination of your true feelings regarding your relationship and your spouse, ask yourself if you can accept certain aspects in your relationship. Your partner and your relationship are not perfect—none of them is—but be honest regarding what you can and cannot accept from the relationship and from your partner. If there are aspects that you cannot accept, and your partner is not willing to compromise or change, you may have to end the relationship. You cannot change another person, no matter how hard you try. If you try to change a person to make you love him or her, you will only make yourself miserable, frustrated, and angry. Sometimes relationships are meant to be, and sometimes they are not. It does not make you a bad person if a relationship fails; it just may be that the two people in the relationship are not meant to be together. Instead of putting energy and time in a relationship that makes you miserable, decide if this relationship is worth saving and then either work on the relationship or move on.

It sounds simple, and I know you love him or her, but remember, love should not make you miserable and unhappy. There is a difference between loving someone and being in love with someone. We love a lot of people, but we don't have sex with them, and we don't want to spend our lives with them in a romantic and intimate way. You have to determine if you love this person or if you are in love with this person. I am not saying that you have to be in love with this person all the time. There are moments when I am not in love with my husband—sometimes I can't stand him. But if someone asks me if I am in love with him most of the time, I would have to say *yes*. I cannot see my life without him, and I truly enjoy being with him and making a life with him. I have loved a lot of people. I have cared for a lot of people, but they are not the people that I want to be lying next to every night. So again, be truthful about your relationship and your partner.

This concept can also be used for your friendships. If you have a friend that constantly causes turmoil and issues, you will have to ask yourself the same questions and determine if you want to be a friend to this person or if you do not. Friends should make your life more enjoyable, not miserable. If you feel as if someone is sucking the life out of you and making you rethink who you are, that is not the friend you want. I have many friends whom I love and enjoy, but if I am putting more energy into the relationship than into myself, there usually is a problem.

If your relationship has become boring and dull, spice it up. Talk to each other, and communicate your thoughts and feelings. More than likely, your partner is feeling the same way. Communicate with your partner in a loving and concerned manner; this can make a big difference in your relationship. Let your partner know that you love him or her and want the relationship to work, but you are bored and need more excitement, one-on-one time, fun together, and love.

Parents/Couples with Children

I know a lot of parents who say they do not have time to be bored because their children keep them busy—with activities, watching them, playing with them, and spending time with them. Children can be very demanding and time-consuming, but I still hear parents say they are bored with their lives. They love their children, but they do not feel fulfilled in their lives. They feel something is missing, or they want more from life. How can this be? How can parents be bored when they are so busy with their children? I realized that I keep myself pretty busy, but I still get bored, so why wouldn't parents with children get bored? They are individual human beings who still have goals, desires, and wants that do not include their children. They still have individual issues, needs, goals, and desires. They still want excitement, love, fulfillment, and passion.

Remember, you have to be *self* before you can be partner and parent. If you are not feeling fulfilled and happy with yourself, and your needs and desires are not being met, you can be the best parent in the world but will still have that nagging feeling of boredom. As a parent, you will be the best role model for your children if you pursue your dreams and goals, while still being involved with their lives and showing them that you can be a person, wife/husband, and parent. You still have to have date night with your spouse or partner. So many couples that come to see me tell me that they do not go on date night because they don't have a babysitter. I will ask them if they have one person they trust to be with their children. Usually, they do, but they feel guilty about leaving their children. I don't know how it feels to leave your child, but I have found that parents who take time for their relationship, even if it is a couple of hours a month, have a healthier and more loving relationship than parents who do not go on dates. Parents need to reconnect with one another and remember why they fell in love with one another.

Another reason couples tell me that they do not go on dates is because they don't have the money. You do not have to have money to go on a date. Go on picnic, go for a long walk or hike, go to the beach, or go pick up McDonald's and find a shady place to sit and eat. You do not need money to go on a date. You have to stay connected so that your relationship will not become boring and stale. You have to remember why you wanted to be together, and get to know each other again and again and again. Being connected to one another is the best gift you can give your children.

Children

What happens when children become bored? This is never good! Nothing drives me crazier than going shopping and hearing a young child crying and whining because the parents have the child out shopping at nine o'clock at night, when the child should be home in bed. The child is tired, bored, and ready to go home. Children who become bored start to whine, act out behaviorally, get involved with activities that they should not, become attention-seeking and—let's face it—bratty. In my experience, most children act out due to boredom and not knowing what to do with themselves. Parents expect their children to sit and behave for a long time, and they usually get mad at their children when they start to act out.

Parents, do not set up your child for failure! You do not do this intentionally, but be mindful of what you are asking your children to do, and honestly ask yourself if they are going to be able to do it. Children do not have to be entertained every minute, but they do need to learn how to entertain themselves. They need to have their own goals, dreams, desires, and activities that they enjoy. They need to have time to themselves to learn how to be creative. They need to learn how to accomplish their own goals and dreams. This can start as young as three years old. While children are learning to become independent, they can also learn how to find creative ways to entertain themselves. Parents should spend time with their children, and they should be role models on how to socialize with others, but they should not be their children's entertainment all the time. Children will get bored, and there are times when parents will not be able to help children with this boredom. They will need to learn how to find ways to occupy themselves that are healthy and creative.

Today, children are more techno-savvy with regard to computers and video games. Their brains are wired much differently than my generation's brains. Children have to learn how to entertain themselves without a computer or electronic device. They have to learn how to interact with one another and socialize. They do not have to be entertained all the time, and they do not have to get their way all the time. Parents have to be parents and not their children's friend. Children have to be disciplined, and they have to have consistent consequences, based on the expectations the parent has for them. They need to know that they are loved and accepted, no matter what they do, but they also have to learn that there are consequences for all their choices and actions. They need to learn how to deal with disappointment and realize that not everyone is equal and not everyone is a winner. They need to learn how to lose and not be a sore loser. They need to learn how to be bored and how to entertain themselves. They need to learn that being bored is "ok" at times and that life is not always entertaining. They need to learn how to accomplish their goals and dreams without someone holding their hand.

Being a parent is the hardest job in the world. It is hard to know when you are doing the right thing for your children. But loving and accepting them, while setting boundaries, expectations, and consequences for them, will be a start on how to teach them to handle this wonderful world and life. By being a role model in life and letting them see you laugh and cry, get angry and frustrated and see you being bored and how you deal with your boredom will be the best example for them.

What about adolescents? When adolescents get bored, what happens? They may throw a temper tantrum—a whole new level of a child's temper tantrum—stomp off, give you the evil look, yell, become defiant, and even throw things. They also look for ways to get their way. They have learned how to manipulate to get what they want. When adolescents get bored, as a parent, you should be concerned. Adolescents will seek out their peers, who will not bore them, and they may seek negative activities, such as drugs and alcohol, to help with their boredom. Ask a teenager why he or she drank that tequila, and 99 percent of the time he or she will say, "I don't know; I was bored." *Bored.* Not a good thing.

You have to keep your children active and involved in activities. This is not a guarantee to having the perfect child that does nothing wrong—no child will ever live up to that expectation—but it will help. It will help to keep children focused on a goal, activity, or hobby. They will usually associate with other children their age who are also active and involved with activities, instead of sitting around doing nothing—or doing something that is not good for them. I am not saying that all teens who are active will not get in trouble, but it does help—but this also has to be balanced. If your children are in too many activities, they will not be bored, but they also will not learn to recognize what they need to do when boredom occurs. They will not have been allowed to be creative and just "be." Adolescents need some time just to learn, sleep, be creative, and get familiar with who they are and what they want to do with their lives. If they are always active, they will not have a chance to do this. Remember, boredom is not always bad, but it needs to be minimal and for short periods. It needs to be balanced between school, activities, being a child, and allowing the child to just "be."

Adolescents are amazing creatures and at times, it is hard to know what they are thinking or doing—hell, half the time they don't understand what they are thinking or doing. While raising my teenage niece, I have had to re-evaluate myself and remember that I too once was a teenager—and not a perfect one. I never got into trouble, but I did things that I should not have done. I was the adolescent who liked to party and have fun but never crossed the line of getting in trouble, mostly due to fear of my mother. Like many parents, I want my niece to have all the opportunities and advantages that I did not have. I find myself wanting to protect her from making mistakes, getting hurt, or doing something wrong. She tells me all the time to let her make her own mistakes so she can learn from them. In my head, I scream *no*, but I know that this will be the only way she really will learn. I just hope she does not make a terrible mistake that will wreck her whole life. She really is a good girl with concrete goals and dreams. She reminds me of me in so many ways, which scares me as she gets older. I don't want her to make the same mistakes I made, and I find myself getting angry with her, when she actually is just being a kid. I have realized she does not have a hobby and is not involved with activities, which has caused her to be bored. She has experimented with drinking alcohol and smoking marijuana, and we have had deep discussion about this. She explained that she was bored, and there was nothing else to do, so she, like many others, found a way not to be bored. I hope that with the open conversations we have had, and with her focus and determination to get a good education and the values and morals we have instilled in her, she will become the person she wants to be, without getting into trouble, making a decision or choice with lifelong ramifications, or hurting herself or someone else. Adolescents need to be able to learn from their decisions and accept the consequences of their behavior. As much as they want too, Mommy and Daddy cannot protect them all the time. Adolescents have to learn something about life on their own. That is what growing up is all about—living and learning.

Boredom and Addictions

When I think of the good and bad experiences I have had in my life, alcohol always seems to be part of those experiences. I would not want to go back to my twenties for anything, but there are times I do want to act like I am twenty-five. I want to dance and drink and not care about the consequences, because that is how I used to act when I was younger. I was lucky that I did not have negative consequences from drinking back then. I am mindful of this every day. But, now that I am older and wiser, I know that I could have big consequences from being under the influence, and I really do not want to take that chance. I cannot drink alcohol like I used to—it's another downfall of getting older. I feel like crap the next day—and the next day and the next day. I am not an alcoholic, but I do like to have a beer or two sometimes. The problem is that the beer does not like me anymore. So I drink wine, but that does not like me either. (Crap, what I am I going to do with myself?) Honestly, up until the past couple of years, my entertainment solely involved drinking alcohol whenever I would go out. Now, I just can't hang like I used too. I am no fun since I stopped drinking. I always got my entertainment from drinking. When I would get bored, I would call my girlfriends and offer beer and wine, and they would come over, which of course caused me not to be bored anymore.

However, now that I'm older and wiser, I don't want to drink as much. I don't find the enjoyment that I used to from getting drunk, acting like a fool, and spending money—and don't even start adding up the calories. Now when I get bored I find creative ways to spend my time, such as cleaning and decorating the house, working out in the yard, TRY to do various arts and craft activities, play golf, take my dog for a walk, exercise, plan a trip and get with my girlfriends for a cocktail or to just talk. When you are bored you have to get yourself doing something, hopefully something that will make you feel good about yourself.

As a substance-abuse counselor, the main topic regarding relapse and recovery is boredom. Many who relapse will report that they were bored. "I had nothing to do, so I got high". Many substance abuser do not want to be in the moment and rather numb themselves so they do not have to deal with daily life and reality. They use substances to deal with their emotional and physical pain. Some who are early in the addiction report getting high because it is "fun and I like the way it makes me feel", but later into their addiction they admit it is not fun anymore, the addiction has taken control over their life. Their main purpose in life is

I am bored and I am TIRED of it!!

getting their "next fix". There are many reason why people get addicted to substances and alcohol, but being bored, not keeping busy and not having direction and goals is what keeps them in their addiction. I work with veterans, many of whom get disability, some of these veterans are very young. Because they are disabled, they do not seek employment, and they have nothing to occupy their time. They are bored, they feel worthless, and they have no direction in their lives. They continue in the cycle of getting clean and sober and then relapsing due to poor coping skills with life situations and being bored. The best thing a person can do for himself or herself when getting clean and sober is get into a routine, have a daily purpose, exercise, work, volunteer, do arts and crafts, or find a hobby—anything that will keep you busy and give you direction for the day.

I am not saying that all substance users and alcoholics are not working and active, but boredom, drug and alcohol usage have a common thread. When I have nothing to do, I will drink a beer or go find my girlfriends and have a glass of wine. If you associate with people who are actively drinking or doing drugs, it will raise the chance that you too will partake in this behavior. As humans, we like to have a commonality and connection with others. We want to fit in so badly with others and at time allow others to influence what we are doing or going to do. The first time I drank alcohol I was in the eighth grade. Me and my best friend were babysitting and we found alcohol and drank it. We laughed and thought it was so much fun—until we got sick. But again, it started off with boredom. Boredom is not effective for recovery. I preach all the time that you have to keep yourself busy, focused, and honest to a have a successful recovery. If you tend to drink alcohol or do illegal substances because you are bored, it is time to self-assess your life and find new ways to relieve your boredom. If you continue to associate with people who are drinking alcohol and doing substance, you may have to stop associating with these people, even if they are family and long term friends. If you live across the street from a bar or your neighbor is your dealer, you may have to move out of the town you live in to distant yourself from people and places that may trigger you to use. You may have to step out of your comfort zone and do activities that are new and different to have a successful recovery, but you will have to be doing "something". Alcohol and illegal substances are not healthy for you and can cause you to have a miserable and difficult life.

When I am busy, I do not have the nagging feeling of being bored or of wanting to do something "wild." Being busy has its benefits, one of which is that you don't have time for the nagging and irrational thoughts that you may have when you have nothing to do. When I was working full-time, going to school three nights a week, and completing my twenty-four-hour-a-week internship, I was not bored and did not have any problems—except lack of sleep. However, after completing school and my internship and only working full-time, I had a whole lot of time to have those thoughts, which now I realize caused some depression for me. I have realized that even though people complain about being busy and tired, they do appear more stable and content with their lives than those who have a lot of time and nothing to do.

A lot of women with children report not having time to focus on anything other than the family. They may not feel completely fulfilled with their lives and may feel like something is missing, but they really don't have a lot of time to think about it. Then the children leave home, and if the mothers are not working or involved with activities, they have a high risk of depression and empty-nest syndrome—they have the time to have irrational thoughts and a possible midlife crisis. Being busy distracts you from feelings and emotions that you may have repressed, but at times it is beneficial to just "be"—just be lazy, just be a couch potato, just be bored. You have to know when it is time to recharge your thoughts, creativity, and energy. When I allow myself to just "be," the next day I feel more focused, energized, and creative. You have to give your time to be bored and do nothing, but this time should only be for short periods. Learn to balance your busy life with a little boredom and doing nothing—yes, nothing! If you are busy all the time, you will burn out and be overwhelmed, but if you are bored all the time, you will lose focus in your life and will probably become depressed, sad, angry, unmotivated, and just miserable. Look at your life and determine if you are balancing your life and making good choices and decisions that will ultimately make you a happier, more fulfilled person.

Chapter 4

························

Boredom and Acknowledgment and Hobbies

························

The two enemies of human happiness are pain and boredom.
—*Arthur Schopenhauer*

Being acknowledged by others is an important aspect in our lives that we do not think much about. *Acknowledgement is the recognition or favorable notice of an act or achievement.* Usually when you are being acknowledge you are getting attention. This acknowledgment/attention can be positive or negative, and it can cause a mixture of emotions, from being happy and proud to being ashamed and embarrassed. Everyone likes to experience positive acknowledgment and attention. Many will say that they don't like being acknowledged and prefer to stay in the background, which is fine, but most people appreciate feeling wanted or needed. They like to be recognized for their accomplishments. Parents like to be proud of their children, and they appreciate hearing how well they've done as parents and how well their children behave. People like to be told that they are loved, beautiful, and nice. Some people like the feeling of being needed by others and like to know that others enjoy their help and company. What if no one cared about you? To be acknowledged means that someone knows you or wants to know you. Being acknowledged is one of the first stages known by psychotherapist Erik Erikson. Babies need to be acknowledged, nurtured, and cared for. If they are not, they will not thrive. It is very important for children to be loved and accepted and to learn how to attach to others and how to respond to others' needs.

Let's say you were not acknowledged, nurtured, or loved as a child. According to Erik Erikson, you will have poor self-esteem, poor self-worth, and you may not know what you want to do with your life. You may pursue love and acknowledgment from people who do not have your best interest in mind, who may hurt or abuse you, and you may engage in drug and alcohol usage to numb your feelings. You may seek out negative acknowledgment, just to get some type of attention. Think about a child who is throwing a temper tantrum. Mother, who is busy doing something, yells at the child to stop, and the child stops for a minute but then starts right back again. Mother again yells at the child to stop. Again the child stops but then starts again. Mother now is very frustrated, and she yells and spanks the child. The child again stops the tantrum, but once Mother is busy again, the child resumes the tantrum. You know what I am talking about—just go into Walmart, and you will hear a child crying and a mother screaming. This child is telling Mom that he/she is bored and wants attention. He/she is not being acknowledged, so this child is going to do anything he can to get the acknowledgment that he deserves. He does not care if it is positive or negative attention; he wants that attention. Now think of this child as a twenty-five-year-old adult who has only received negative attention for his behavior. What do you think he is going to do when he wants attention? He is going to act like a five-year-old, but now he may be more violent or self-destructive in his attempts to get attention.

I am not saying that you have to give your children attention 24/7 or that you have to acknowledge their presence 24/7, but you do have to acknowledge their behavior. You cannot ignore their good behavior, and you definitely cannot ignore their bad behavior. It is easy to turn away from your child and not acknowledge negative behaviors, but what about their positive behaviors? They have to know that when they do something good, they will be acknowledged and rewarded. They need to feel loved, accepted, and appreciated. Acknowledging their positive behaviors can make the difference in how your children grow and treat others when they become adults. It can make a difference in their self-esteem and self-worth. You do not have to go overboard with the reward or acknowledgment of their achievements and good behavior. Even a simple "I am proud of you" or "thank you" can make a huge difference and is more positive than not being acknowledged at all.

What happens when a child continues to present bad or negative behaviors? I have told parents to ignore their child's negative behaviors—and by "ignore," I mean they should not entertain this behavior. So many times, parents get caught up in lecturing, yelling, smacking, or just ignoring (which can put fuel on the fire of the behavior) their children when they are acting up. We entertain our children by the way we act towards them. Children want attention, good or bad. When we entertain our children with our display of attention, they feed off of this. It fulfills them.

I hear parents say all the time that if they ignore their child's bad behavior, the child will stop doing it. Sometimes this works, and yes, I have recommended to parents to not acknowledge this bad behavior. You cannot ignore it, however, and expect your child to understand what you are doing. You do have to set boundaries and expectations with your children so that they will understand. You have to acknowledge your children's positive behaviors so they learn that such behavior is accepted and makes you happy. If a child comes home happy and excited because he got all As on his report card, and you do not acknowledge this great accomplishment, then more than likely this child will not feel that this is a good accomplishment and will give up. If you acknowledge this child's accomplishment with praise, appreciation, and pride, he will feel good about himself and continue to want to get the praise and good feelings of making you proud. Liking that feeling of accomplishment should continue throughout the child's lifetime.

I am bored and I am TIRED of it!!

As a teen I was always grounded for the grades on my report card. I was not failing classes, but my mother felt I was not putting enough effort into my grades. One semester, I put a lot of effort and time into my schoolwork and came home with all As and Bs and one C. This was a great accomplishment for me, but when I came home, proud of my report card, I still got grounded for getting the one C. I was angry and frustrated. I did not receive any positive acknowledgment for my good grades; the focus was on the one lower grade. So what did I do? I became defiant. I decided if I was going to be grounded for that C, then I might as well fail all my subjects. It did not matter if I got the best grades I could get or if I failed everything—I was still going to be grounded. So the next semester, I got Ds and Fs, and yes, I got grounded. I expected to get grounded and in trouble for these grades, and I did not care. After my mother and I had a long talk, and I was able to explain how I felt, she started to acknowledge the good grades, and I was not grounded anymore. And guess what? I went to college and completed by bachelor's and master's degrees. I kept going to school to feel good about my accomplishments and to make my mother proud of me.

How does acknowledgment relate to boredom? Think about it: if you are bored, are you being acknowledged? Are those around you acknowledging your presence by engaging you in conversation or in activities? Let's look at that five-year-old again. Let's say he has been at the store with his mother for two hours. For most of the two hours, he was able to entertain himself, but then he started to get bored. He tried, in his child language, to tell his mother he was bored. Mother did not listen, so he acted out, and Mother shows him attention (acknowledging his behavior), which makes him feel okay for a minute. Then the boredom comes back, so he acts out again, but this time he's louder. What does Mom do? She gets louder and pays him more attention (acknowledging the behavior). You can see where I am going with this, right?

If Mom knows, however, that a five-year-old's attention span is between three and seven minutes, she will make sure he will have some entertainment. She makes sure he has a game or something to keep him occupied for a little while. She may promise him that if he behaves himself, she will play a game with him when they get home. She also knows, however, that shopping for two hours with a five-year-old is out of the question, and she may take a break from shopping after about an hour to take him to the park to play for thirty minutes. There are a hundred ways to handle this situation of the child crying and the mother screaming. What does the child learn from this scenario? When a child is bored, he will make sure you know it. He will do whatever he can to get your attention. He will learn that by acting out, he will get some attention, even if it is negative attention. Children learn that any attention is good attention, and they will act any way they can to get that attention. The first time I asked the question "Were you acknowledged as a child by your parents, teachers, and peers?" to a group of men who were referred to my group due to domestic violence, I found it alarming that many of my them reported that they did not feel acknowledged as children. The only time they got attention was when they misbehaved. They reported not feeling accepted or part of their family. This got me thinking about how important it is to be acknowledged, accepted and to feel a part of your family and peer group.

We all want to be a part of something, to know that we are loved, accepted, and appreciated. Think about your childhood, and ask yourself the following questions:

- When I walked into a room, did anyone acknowledge that I was there, or did they ignore me?
- Were my parents emotionally present when I was having a difficult time?
- When I misbehaved, what did my parents do?
- Did I feel wanted by my family?

You may wonder how this has anything to do with boredom. Well, it has a lot to do with it. If you were a child who was ignored or not acknowledged, what kind of behaviors did you do to get attention? Act out, misbehave, act like a brat, or withdraw and isolate? Any of these behaviors are not healthy, especially for children and especially during childhood and adolescence, when they are learning how to socialize and get along with others, as well as learning how to manipulate and get what they want. If children learn that they only way to get attention and to relieve their feeling of boredom is to misbehave, there is a good chance that this is the behavior they will show as an adult. You learn skills that will manifest, when you are an adult, into behaviors that are attention-seeking and impulsive. If you start to feel bored, unwanted, unloved, and unaccepted, you will seek out ways to get the attention that you are craving, one way or another.

It is human behavior to seek attention, acknowledgment, love, and nurturance. Really think about this—not just when you were a child but also as an adult. Think about how the lack of acknowledgment may be affecting your relationships, your work performance, your attitude toward others, and your self-esteem. Exam how you acknowledge your own children and other loved ones. Show them that you love, appreciate, and accept them, and see how this improves your relationship.

Boredom vs. Hobby

I have found that people with hobbies are happier and more fulfilled. A hobby is defined as a regular activity that is done for pleasure, typically, during one's leisure time. My coworker has several hobbies, and she explained that she is never bored. "What is boredom?" she asked. People who have an activity that they enjoy appear more focused and content with their lives. They have something that fills their time, and they feel more creative and accomplished. A hobby can be anything that is healthy for you and that makes you happy. You do need to balance your hobby with the rest of your life, such as job, relationships, and children, or your hobby can become unhealthy. You have to prioritize your hobbies and your responsibilities. Many people make their hobbies the priority and then wonder why other aspects of their lives fall apart. If my husband could have one dream, it would be to play professional golf. He loves playing golf, and we have had several come-to-Jesus moments regarding what is more important to him—golf, me, or his career. He has been able to balance his career, relationship and hobby in a way that allows him to still take responsibility for his career and relationship, but he takes time to do an activity that he absolutely enjoys. I have found that men seem to have more hobbies than women have. If I ask thirty men what their hobbies are, they mention very different hobbies—playing different sports, restoring old cars, tinkering in their shed, exercise, fishing, hunting. If I ask thirty women what their hobbies are, sadly, most of them will explain that their children are their hobbies, or they don't have an individual hobby. Of course, some are able to identify hobbies that they used to have—exercise, metal detecting, painting, sports, shopping—but for the most part, women in their thirties and forties have lost interest in their hobbies. Some women explain that they do not have a hobby, but they still keep themselves busy by spending time with friends, watching TV, taking pictures of their children, and cleaning the house. They feel content with doing these things and don't feel bored. I have explained to them that even though they do not have a "hobby," they are taking personal responsibility for their actions, decisions, and life by doing activities that make them content and fulfilled. Remember, you don't always have to have something to do—sometimes it is nice not to have anything to do—but a hobby or doing something you enjoy will make you a healthier person.

I have tried different activities with my husband—golfing, hunting, shooting—but I become bored! I love trying new activities, and I am pretty open to suggestions, but if I do not find it interesting, then it will not be an activity that fills my soul or boredom. I always encourage client's to try an activity once before making the decision that they don't like it. Try to participate in activities that your friend and/or partner likes to do. At least try it once! If you really want to make your partner happy, try it a couple of times and put in a positive effort to enjoy it.

My husband is excited when I play golf with him, but he learned to accept that I get bored after the first nine holes. We have learned to compromise. He appreciates that I play nine holes, and that makes a difference in our relationship. I have also tried shooting guns. I hate guns, but I enjoy it when I go. It's not very often, but I know he likes it. In turn, he knows I like animals, so he will go to the zoo or pet store with me (reluctantly, but he will go). This is what compromising looks like: doing things that you really don't like to do, but you will do because your partner likes it. And you never know—you just might like the activity and will want to continue to do it!

Chapter 5

My Experiences with Personal Responsibility

There's no excuse to be bored. Sad, yes. Angry, yes. Depressed, yes. Crazy, yes. But there's no excuse for boredom, ever.
—Viggo Mortensen

When I was sixteen years old, I started working in a little convenience store down the street from my house. This was the local hangout, so I liked this job—I was able to see my friends when they came in. I stayed there for about a year and then moved on to working at the mall in a clothing store, which I also loved—I got discounts on clothes and again was able to see my friends. With both of these jobs, I did not like being told that I had to work when I did not want to do so. I would quit, but I was always able to get a new job pretty quickly. I started working in the restaurant business as a hostess/waitress. I loved this type of work; I was able to socialize and have a flexible schedule. Here again, however, I did not like it when I was told that I had to work when I'd rather be with my friends. I worked at about ten restaurants during a three-year period. I always had a job, and I had a good work ethic—when I was at work and when the schedule was to my liking. I often have asked myself what direction my life would have gone if I'd continued with this pattern of leaving jobs as an adult. As I got older, however, I did become more focused on the concept that if I wanted nice things, then I needed to get a job and stay in that job, even when I did not want to work. If you think about it, who *really* wants to work, especially forty-plus hours a week? Nobody!

While attending college, I worked two part-time jobs, as a waitress and in the child-care industry, which was good experience. Once I completed my bachelor's degree, I got my first real social work job, working with children who had been abused and neglected. This was an eye-opening experience, seeing how the parents behaved toward their children. During an eight-hour shift, it was not unusual for another coworker and I to have to restrain a child or adolescent because he or she had threatened to hurt us or himself/herself. Parents of these children were relatively nonexistent, and when they were present, they only intensified the children's behaviors. After leaving this position, I started to work with Child Protective Services and Foster Care. I did this job for almost five years, which also was great experience; it allowed me to become the social worker I am today. As a child protective services/foster care social worker I saw a lot of bad in people but also a lot of good. I saw and heard parents do things to their children that were unimaginable. I wondered why people had children if they couldn't take care of them and treat them with basic care.

Eventually, I got "burned out" in the social work field and decided to teach elementary school—second and third grade. When the school system saw my résumé, they were happy to give this social worker three years to get a teaching license. I started right away with teaching third grade at an at-risk school. I taught for two years and then realized that I was still doing social work but also having to educate these children. I realized very quickly that I was much better as a social worker than as a teacher. This was the point in my life when I started to question if I really wanted children. I went back to school to complete my master's in social work and started working as an in-patient psychiatric social worker. I absolutely loved this job and had great mentoring and support. At first, I was hesitant to work on a closed/locked unit with the mentally ill, but I found them fascinating and entertaining. (Remember, I like to be entertained!) After completing my master of social work degree and going through an emotional divorce, I decided to leave my job and move to a new area. I see now that I was running away. I moved from my hometown and lived on my own for the first time ever. I had a great studio apartment and got a job as a supervisor for an intensive foster care program. I was there for three months, during which time I met my current husband, who was living, ironically, back in my hometown. Obviously, I moved back to my hometown and got my job back at the hospital as a medical social worker, working on the oncology unit. This was a new experience, as I never had seen anybody die. The first person I saw pass away due to cancer was a seventeen-year-old male who had been diagnosed only two months before he died. It was horrible. Within that year, my husband and I got married, and my husband, who is active duty in the Air Force, moved to Hawaii. I was excited and scared at the same time. I got the opportunity to work for a nonprofit agency, working with the mentally ill homeless population in Hawaii. I loved this job—I was in Hawaii, wearing shorts and slippers (flip-flops for you non-Hawaiians), walking along the beaches, and helping the mentally ill, who of course entertained and fascinated me. I also completed my licensed clinical social work (LCSW) requirements, took the test three times, and finally passed, all by my stated goal of completing my LCSW by age thirty-five. What a great experience! That is when I started to write this book. While working with the homeless, I started a weekly cognitive group on responsibility, and that is when I started to put all my experiences together. Because my husband is in the military, he encouraged me to get into the federal system, which I did, and that is what I am doing now.

Why have I shared this with you? I wanted you to see that through all my professional experiences as a social worker and teacher, I found a common aspect with all the people I worked with—they were bored or did not have any goals or motivation. Most of my clients, whether children or adults, did not know how to take control of their lives and did not have any self-worth to accomplish their dreams, causing them to do basically *nothing*. Doing nothing equals boredom, which leads to depression, substance and alcohol abuse, obesity, low self-esteem, anger, resentment—the list can go on and on. This was the common theme to people who were not living a healthy, happy, and fulfilled life.

When I started working in the mental health/substance-abuse profession, I had the same feelings and perceptions as most of society—why are "these" people not taking care of themselves? Why are they relying on medications, government, jail system, family, and other agencies to take care of them? Why are there so many people blaming others for their actions? Why are we, as a society, allowing people to blame others for their actions? Have you heard someone say that he or she was going to sue an agency or a person because the agency did not help the person? At one time or another, everyone has felt mistreated by an agency, by a stranger, or by someone they know. Everyone has had this experience; it is not a good experience, but it happens. How we handle this experience is the key to taking responsibility for our lives and having a fulfilled and purposeful life. The choices that we make every second, minute, hour, and day determine the direction of our lives. As humans, we are all going to make bad choices, and we are all going to make good choices. When we make good choices, we like to pat ourselves on the back and high-five everyone, but when we make bad choices, we are expected to get sad, depressed, and feel horrible about ourselves. This is wrong. Taking responsibility for our bad choices is just as important, if not more important, than taking responsibility for the good choices that we have made.

We need to learn from the choices we make every day—that is what learning is about. If everyone made good choices every day and was living a wonderful and carefree life, this world would be perfect. We know, however, that this is not happening. Learning from the choices in our lives and taking responsibility for them is the key to a fulfilling life. My motto is live and learn. We need to learn from our mistakes, or problems will continue to arise, as we will continue to make wrong choices over and over again. Learn from your mistakes and move forward in your life. Live and learn.

Fortunately, my mother taught me throughout my life how to take responsibility for my actions and that I should not rely on others to take care of me. I did not like this concept; in fact, I still do like to blame others for my misfortunes. I have realized in this profession, however, that I was lucky to learn to take responsibility for my actions. Many are not so lucky. Throughout my professional experience in the social services agencies, court systems, school systems, nonprofit agencies, medical and mental health and homeless agencies, I have seen that we, as a society, are not taking responsibility for ourselves or for each other. Look at our government—they are not learning from their mistakes, and they are not taking responsibility for their choices, actions, and decisions. They continue to blame each other and everyone else for the corruption and misguidance of our country. When our government shows this type of behavior, the ripple effect occurs among the systems and programs under the government. Each professional system blames the other professional system. Each person blames another person for not getting needs meets. Society makes excuses for everyone's actions and does not hold people accountable. For example, the gun laws—blame the guns, not the person who is holding the gun. The mental health system is in a state of crisis, but this seems not to matter to the leaders of this country, even though time and time again, someone with a mental illness hurts himself or someone else. This is a good example of not taking personal responsibility. We all have to be held to a standard and be accountable for our actions and for the systems that are created to help those who cannot take responsibility for their thoughts and actions.

I am a firm believe that even if you do have a mental illness, it is still your responsibility to get the help and support that will allow you to function in society. If you are not able to do this, then someone you trust needs to be appointed as a guardian to help you have a life that will allow you and others to be safe.

So my question is this: what if you do not take responsibility for your actions and continue to blame others for your misfortunes? What positive attributes can come from this mentality? I hope you recognize and acknowledge that if you continue to blame others, you are not taking responsibility for your life, and you are not learning from your mistakes. Blaming others is a learned behavior that causes you to reflect all your bad thoughts and feelings about yourself toward another. If you continue to participate in this behavior, you will live a life of unhappiness, loneliness, anger, regret, resentment toward others, boredom, and depression. How can boredom occur if you blame others? For example, you blame others for not accomplishing your goals. It is everyone else's fault that you did not finish your degree or get a good job. It is someone else's fault that you are bored and not doing anything. If you continue to think this way, you will stop trying. You will lose any passion for what you want to do, which will lead to what? *Boredom.* You have to be honest with yourself, and point the finger back at yourself instead of at others, if you want to accomplish anything. Answer the following questions truthfully and write out the answers. Then read them back to yourself. This will allow you to see what you wrote and to determine for yourself if you have answered the questions truthfully.

How often do you allow others to make decisions for you?
How easy is it to blame others for where you are today?
How easy is it to accept blame or admit mistakes?
How often do you depend on others to feel good about yourself?
Do you feel good about who you are and what you are doing in your life?
How frequently do you feel sorry for yourself?
How many masks do you hide behind so that you present as a certain person in different situations?

The last question regarding the masks you wear is a very important question. If you find yourself trying to present yourself as a different person in every situation or with different people or different environments, then you are not being honest with yourself. Do you really know who you are if you are wearing multiple masks? For example, if you go to work every day and present yourself as a kind person, but then you go home and beat your wife and children, you are presenting as two different people. I understand you may act differently when you are at work than when you are out with your friends for dinner. When you are at work, you are expected to act professionally and more reserved, but when you are with family and friends, you can let loose and let your hair down. The difference is that you are still the same person, just acting in a way that is expected of you. We all act differently in different setting, but do you still treat people the same, and do you still remain true to who you are in both setting? Do you still display the same beliefs, morals, and values? Here's another example I give regarding masks: I have a friend who changes everything about herself every time she gets involved in a new relationship. She changes her hair, what she likes to do, what music she listens to, and even her friends. She eventually gets frustrated with the man she is dating—I believe this is due to her putting on a new mask to please her new boyfriend. She loses herself, which eventually causes her to become frustrated and angry, causing the relationship to end. Changing her true self to please others is not healthy. I have a lot of faults, but I always say, "What you see is what you get." The way you see me at work (a little more professional) is the same person you will see at the store. Please think about the masks you may wear, and think about the reason you are wearing these masks. Which mask do you really want to wear? Who do you really want to be?

Chapter 6

Taking Responsibility for Your Life

Only those who want everything done for them are bored.
—Billy Graham

As a social worker, I have found that I cannot control or tell people what they should be doing with their life. I can help direct and support, but I cannot drive the car to their happiness. Everyone has responsibility for their lives, and what they choose to do or not do is up to them.

When I first started doing a weekly support group with homeless individuals, they would ask me what the topic was for the group. I would say, "It's 'How to Take Responsibility for Your Life.'" They would look at me and say, "No, I don't think I want to attend this group." I would encourage them to come, and some did, and of course some did not. The ones who attended stated that the topic of taking "responsibility" for their life was not what they thought it would mean. Most of the members who attended this group liked this topic and understood the concept; however, reported barriers to why they have not been able to take responsibility. Most of these barriers dealt with past trauma, abuse, abandonment from loved ones, drug and alcohol dependency, relationship issues, the federal and state programs, and the fact that they did not know how to take responsibility, because they had never been held accountable for their actions or choices. I use the word "choices" all the time, and now I even have clients who tell me, "I made the choice of ..." This is a big step toward taking responsibility for their lives. Taking responsibility for your boredom is a choice you can make. It is ultimately your responsibility to make changes and empower yourself to have the life you want.

I like to use the phrase, you are being responsible when you accept that *you* choose the direction of your life. In my weekly support group with homeless individuals who have mild mental illness and substance and alcohol dependency, I explain that I could have easily been in their shoes. My mother and father separated when I was seven years old, due to my father's alcoholism. When I was nine years old, my father committed suicide, leaving my mother to be a single parent to me and my older brother and sister. Throughout my adolescence, I experimented with alcohol and marijuana. I was not doing very well in school and the only hobby that interested me was partying. The direction of my life was heading towards alcoholism, drinking and driving and not doing anything positive with my life. When I was about seventeen years old, however, something in my life changed, and I started looking towards a different direction.

My peers were going away to college and having a great time. I would visit my friends in college and would think, *This is where I want to be*. I admit that partying was the key factor to wanting to go away to college, but that changed once I was there. I thought life should be fun and exciting, and I decided that I did want to go away to college, even for the wrong reason. However, making this decision caused me to improve my grades so I could get into college, find employment to pay for college, and to decide on how to make a career for myself. I experienced several barriers to achieving this goal. My first barrier was not getting accepted into college my first year due to my grades, but instead of focusing on this barrier, I attended my first year at a community college. From there, I was accepted into a university and began my journey into the social work field.

I still stumbled here and there with my grades and with choosing to go out with friends rather than study, but after five years, I did complete my bachelor's degree and swore I would never go back to school again. However, three years later, I was applying for the master of social work program. This process was not a free ride, and I am still paying student loans to this day. I have heard individuals say they cannot afford to go to college or any higher education program. Let me tell you: this is not true. If you really want to go to college, there are financial programs that will assist you with grants or low-rate student loans, so do not let this hold you back. It comes down to your motivation and the choices you make to succeed in life. During this period of my life, I was not bored—I was too busy. Life was flying by me at a rapid speed, and I did not have time to be bored. I felt focused and motivated to accomplish my goals.

During this time, I was growing and learning constantly. I made several bad mistakes, which haunt me from time to time. I have regrets and moments when I think back to my twenties and ask myself, "What was I thinking?" But you cannot go back to your past and beat yourself up about what you did or did not do when you were younger. You can only learn from these experiences and move forward in life. Growing up, we all have had good and bad experiences. We can look back through our lives and think of people who have been important figures and who have guided us through the good and difficult times. Some people will stand out in our memory because they were not good, were not healthy for us, and they did not have our best interests.

I have many memories of stupid behaviors that I choose to participate in. There are days that I thank God for still being alive. Every experience we have growing up does affect us, one way or another, as adults. People get tired of a therapist asking about their childhood, but there is a logical and important reason for this. Your past makes you the person you are today. It molds who you are and who you will become. For example, I have an older brother and sister. We have the same parents and were raised by both of them. The choices I have made in my life are very different from the choices my older brother and sister made. They were eighteen and sixteen years old when my father and mother separated and my father passed away. They saw my mother and father argue more than I did, and they also saw my father drinking and doing drugs. My mother was stricter on them and had higher expectations of them. When my siblings were younger my mom was very resentful and angry with my father, and would project her negative feelings on my siblings. She was not physically abusive toward them, but there are questions about her not being emotionally available for their needs. My father passed away when I was nine years old. My mother was working, and my siblings were living on their own. It was just my mom and me, so we were closer, and she was there for me emotionally. As my siblings and I got older, we talked about why I made such different choices and choose different goals than they did. This goes back to how family dynamics and interactions can affect you as an adult. Even when we try to forget or distance ourselves from the negative family drama, it still follows you and creeps up to present itself. I feel that our childhood past is like a pimple that grows and becomes infected and then eventually pops. As an adult, it is very important to deal with any past issues that may not be positive, because it will affect you as an adult.

Taking responsibility for your life means being able to live with the choices that you make. I have made choices that make me angry and resentful, but I have learned to deal with them and move on. There is nothing I can do about my past. I can't change it, and it will never go away, but I have realized that I need to learn from my past and move forward in my future. The key is to not make the same mistakes over and over. When you continue to make the same mistakes, you are not being truthful with yourself, and you are not learning and growing. Embrace these past experiences, and look at ways you can learn from them.

Responsibility and making choices is not all about making decisions about drugs and drinking alcohol, going to college, or having children. It is also about not feeling sorry for yourself, for taking care of your health and emotional well-being, for looking at yourself in an honest light and knowing who you are and what you stand for in this world.

It is about acknowledging and understanding your purpose in this life. You have the ultimate decision of letting go of blame, anger, sadness, and frustration by being aware of how others have treated you and how you treated others.

As we get older, we are able to understand our past with more clarity and acceptance. We have our own experiences and we have made our own mistakes and realize no one is perfect. We are able to see and accept why people have acted or done things that at first did not seem very nice or logical. We have a tendency to focus on our childhood and hold onto what our parents did or did not do for us when we were younger, hell some of us as adults still focus on what our parents are doing or not doing for us. We want to blame our parents for our mistakes as adults. I have been able see my parents through adult eyes and realize that they are human and made mistakes. I have been able to let go of resentful feelings because I realize that they might not have known how to be better parents. They were going through their own crisis of dealing with life and their dysfunctional marriage. I have come to terms with the fact that my father committed suicide and left his family. He chose to leave his wife and children. He chose not to see us grow up and have our own lives and families. He made a selfish choice, but it was his choice, He will never know what he has missed out on. Why should I allow this to affect me as an adult when he is the one missing out on his family and life? I do have my moments of anger because my father was not man enough to protect and take care of his family and I grew up without a father, But again, he made this decision, not me. We need to let go of blaming our parents and those who are in our lives. You are an adult and you have the ability to make your own decisions and choices, your parents are no longer, or should no longer, be making decisions in your life. Again, you may ask them for advice or for their opinion, but you have to make the final decision and stop blaming others for the direction of *your* life.

When I am bored and have no direction in my life, these are the thoughts I have. They make me angry and resentful, so why do I go back to these thoughts? At times, it is healthy to reflect on the past and determine how it has made me the person I am today. Reflect on what you have learned from your past, so you can move forward in your future. But be careful with dwelling on your past and allowing your past to cause your present and future to be unhealthy. You cannot change your past, but you can determine your future.

What does taking responsibility for your decisions and choices have to do with being bored? First, you have to be able to recognize that your boredom is a manifestation of your thoughts. You are only bored if you allow yourself to be bored. You are choosing to be bored. There are thousands of activities in which you can choose to participate that will help alleviate your boredom, but it is your responsibility to take action and make it happen. No one is going to entertain you or tell you what to do. Boredom and personal responsibility are entwined with one another, and *you* will have to make changes in your thought process to have a healthier, fulfilled, and happy life.

Chapter 7

Why You May Not Be Taking Responsibility for Your Life

To do the same thing over and over again is not only boredom: it is to be controlled by rather than to control what you do.
—Heraclitus

Why should you take responsibility for your life? Well, why would you *not* want to take responsibility for your life? It is your life—all yours and no one else's. You are the person who has to deal with all the good and bad things in your life. Again, I am going to say that we all have had good and bad events happen to us, and no one is perfect. So let's discuss a couple of events that can prevent you from wanting to take responsibility and to give up on being in control of your life.

Trauma

If you have had a traumatic experience, then you know how hard it is to take responsibility or control of your actions. If someone has violated you or done something hurtful or unexpected to you, then you are a victim. A victim of abuse is different from your doing something to yourself or others. As a victim, you need to take responsibility on how you are going to react to the situation. *React* means how you are going to take care of yourself through this tough situation. When we are victims of a traumatic situation, we usually lose control. We go through many emotions of anger, guilt, denial, sadness, and helplessness. We question ourselves and ask why; how could this happen to me? Could I have done something different? We go through the could have, should have, would haves. This is normal behavior, but it can become very unhealthy. We cannot go back in time and change the past, but we can influence the future. How we respond to a traumatic event will help how we move forward in our lives. I am not saying you shouldn't get upset, cry, scream, yell, curse, or stay in bed, but don't allow yourself to do this for a long time. Allow yourself a day or two to process—cry, get angry, sleep, yell, isolate yourself—but after a day or two, it is time to move on and start back with your life. You may need help and support from friends, family, and a professional therapist, but you need to get up and move on.

If you have been physically, verbally, or sexually abused, raped, or assaulted, then you have experienced a wide range of emotions. Any type of abuse by another person is commonly identified with power. A person who is abusive in any form is trying to get power in his or her life, and this is the only way that the person knows how to get this control. If you allow another person to abuse you, you give that person power and control. Once you stop the abuse, leave the person abusing you, or fight back, you are taking this power and control away from him or her and are empowering yourself and taking control of your life. Remember, if anyone is going to be a power and control freak, let it be you, and let it be you taking power of *your* life. This may sound simple, but it is very hard to take control of your life if you are in an abusive situation; you likely have feelings of fear and self-doubt. If you are in an abusive situation, please get help and support before taking control of your life. Support is the key to becoming empowered and safe.

If you have witnessed a traumatic event or have been involved in an event in which you did not want to be a part, this too can cause you trauma.

I want to focus on the military active duty and veterans. As a social worker working with active-duty and veteran military men and women, I've seen that the hardest hurdle for those who have been in combat is to forget what they have witnessed or experienced. More and more military veterans are being diagnoses with post-traumatic syndrome disorder (PTSD), due to having flashbacks, nightmares, and hypervigilency when in a crowded area; they continue to relive their experience. They are unable to stop thinking about what they saw or who they may have hurt while in battle. If they witnessed someone dying, they have a hard time not feeling that they could have helped this person or that the person who died should have been them. These types of traumatic events affect not only military but also civilians who have witnessed similar incidents in their yards or homes or within the community. If you are having these symptoms, please contact a trained mental health specialist who specializes in PTSD. There is hope for PTSD, and there are good treatments that will allow you to work through the traumatic events and have a functional life again. Again, you have to make the decision to get this help. Don't allow the PTSD to take over your life; take control over the PTSD.

There are several types of traumatic events that may occur in your life, although what I assume is a traumatic event, another may not. How I handle a traumatic event may be very different from another person. Be honest with yourself on what is causing you stress, anxiety, depression, boredom, and guilt. With any traumatic event, the first step is getting help by talking about it, recognizing it as a traumatic event, and then learning how to cope with it. You have to empower yourself to get through the emotions and nightmares. Again, you have to take control of your life, instead of the emotions and nightmares taking control of you. This is not easy, and again I encourage you to get more intensive therapeutic treatment to address this so that you *can* move forward in your life.

Fear

This is such a strong feeling. I believe that fear is the one emotion that can stop you in your tracks and keep you from moving. When a person is fearful about making a decision or taking a chance on an opportunity, then he or she is at risk of living a lonely, unhealthy, unworthy, and boring life. Several clients have said to me that they were afraid that they would fail again. My reaction is, "So what?" So what if you fail, as long as you keep trying, because eventually you will succeed. If you stop trying, you have given up!

While studying for my LCSW exam, I experienced anxiety and fear of failing the exam and looking stupid at my job. Due to this fear and anxiety, I failed the exam twice. Even though I know social work is the career for me, I was ready to give up on my clients, change profession, and never work again. I was a mess. However, a couple of days after taking the exam, I regrouped, got angry at myself for being such a coward, began studying again, and finally, on the third try, I passed. I did not let my fear of failing stop me; actually, it made me want to prove to myself that I could pass and could be the best social worker that I could be. Everyone fears something, even macho men who say that they are not afraid of anything. Fears can range from a fear of an insect to a fear of leaving your house.

The best way to overcome fear is to confront it head on—although this is admittedly easier said than done. If your fears are stopping you from succeeding in your life, then take the responsibility of confronting it in order to move forward. Don't let your fear stop you. If anything, get mad at that fear and tell it that you will not let it take control of your life— you will overcome the fear. As you answer the following questions, you may be able to identify several fears. You may fear failure, commitment, success, social obligations, planes, cars, spiders, snakes (my fear), your house, your family, or just yourself. This list can go on and on. Identify all your fears and answer each question for each fear:

1. What are you afraid of?
2. How is the fear stopping you from accomplishing a goal or dream?
3. What can you do to get over this fear?

Fear is nothing to be ashamed of, but you have to identify your fear, acknowledge it, and eventually overcome it, especially if it is having a negative impact on your life and happiness. Take control, and move forward in your life.

Shame and Pride

We all have done things that we are not proud about. We feel ashamed by what we may have said or done and who we may have hurt. We feel ashamed, so we try to avoid whatever we feel bad about. However, if you allow your shame and pride to hold you back from doing what you want to do or talking to someone you want to talk to, you allow your negative feeling to take over your life. For example, a father has not seen his child for a long time and feels ashamed for not calling or talking to her. Due to this shame, he avoids her and does not try to connect with her. He thinks about this often, usually when he lies down to go to sleep, and it brings negative feelings and thoughts about him and about his capacity as a father. Years go by, and he runs into his daughter, and all those negative thoughts come up. He does not know what to say; he walks away feeling worse. If this father had swallowed his pride years ago and admitted to himself and daughter that his behavior was not very fatherly, he could have had a relationship with his daughter, but he did not. This cycle will continue, and he will continue to feel bad about himself, because he is not taking responsibility for his actions and his feelings. My suggestion to this father would be to talk or visit with daughter and tell her, "I am so ashamed of the way I have been as a father." By acknowledging this feeling, he may be surprised by how his daughter reacts and understands.

Shame Regarding Drug Usage

While doing my weekly substance-abuse groups, "shame" is mentioned often. Members openly discuss the shame they feel regarding what they did when they were high or when they were trying to get their fix. This shame can eat them alive and cause severe depression and anxiety. You have to acknowledge this shame and deal with it. The eighth and ninth step with the AA twelve-step program encourages alcoholics to make a list of all the people they have harmed and to make amends by admitting how they hurt them. This is taking responsibility for your actions. This is acknowledging how your behavior hurt someone. This is a good first step towards making amends with those you love and want in your life. You are taking responsibility for your actions. This is one of the hardest steps, because you have to acknowledge what you have done and tell someone you're sorry. You have to swallow your pride and admit your weaknesses and your feelings. And you are not guaranteed that these people will forgive you, but this is a step toward taking responsibility for your actions and attempting to put your past behind you so that you can move forward. Shame and pride can poison any relationship. You have to know when it is time to swallow you pride, put aside your shame, and admit your faults. Most of the time, when you put aside your shame and pride, you allow yourself to become vulnerable.

Being Vulnerable

Many people do not like being vulnerable—they think it means being weak. When you open yourself up to others and allow them to see your true self, you become vulnerable. This is hard for most people to do because of past experiences of rejection. Rejection, especially to adolescents, is emotionally devastating. In my practice, I ask my clients, "What is the one trigger that makes you want to use substances or drink alcohol?" The first answer is usually boredom, but the next trigger is being rejected. Vulnerability and rejection can go hand in hand and can be devastating. Think about it—if everyone lived behind their pride and insecurities and did not show a vulnerable side, how could any relationship be successful? Sometimes you have to make the choice to swallow your pride and be vulnerable in order to learn more about who you are and to open yourself to a new relationship or to mend old relationships. I am not saying that you have to be an open book and allow everyone to know everything about you, but you will have to make the choice of allowing people into your life and see the real you, the positive—and even the negative—characteristics that make you the person you are. Not everyone will like you, but that is okay. It is okay if not everyone likes you. It is okay if people know your faults. The people who know your faults, fears, and insecurities and love you anyway are the people you want in your life. You will have to establish boundaries with people and people will have to earn your respect and trust before you allow them in your life, but you will have to allow others into your life. You will have to be vulnerable at times, you will have to swallow your pride and you will have to admit your fears and weaknesses, if you want to have positive relationships and true understanding of yourself.

Chapter 8

What Can Occur If You Do Not Take Responsibility for Your Life

I fear the boredom that comes with not learning and not taking chances.
—Robert Fulghum

Several factors can happen when you do not take responsibility for your life. You will find yourself in a sticky web, unable to move. You may find yourself being dependent on others or on substances and/or alcohol. You will find yourself having irrational thoughts about yourself and your life. You will develop defense mechanisms that will become unhealthy and irrational. You will become complacent and *bored*—yes, we are going back to how boredom can affect your life. But there is hope! No matter how old you are, no matter what gender or color, or what the situation may be, you have a choice to make a change, even though it may not be easy.

My clients often ask, "Why should I take responsibility for my life?" Most of these individuals are people who have suffered trauma. Most of these people have been abused physically, sexually, or emotionally by those they trusted and loved and who should have protected them from harm. Some of these individuals have seen generation after generation rely on governmental systems and other agencies to take care of their needs. Responsibility is not an instinct that we are born with; this is a learned behavior. If you are not taught this behavior, then you cannot understand the concept of taking care of yourself.

I try to explain the following concepts with regard to not taking control or responsibility over your life. Not taking responsibility for your life can lead to boredom, codependency, fears, and irrational thoughts that will eventually stop you from enjoying your life.

Codependency

By not taking responsibility for your life, you may become overly dependent on others. If you are dependent on others, you are unable to take control of your life and live a life that is fulfilling for you. When we rely on others for recognition, approval, affirmation, or acceptance, we are basically giving others our puppet strings, to control us and tell us what to do, how to act, and how to feel. Have you ever asked a person, "What should I do?" I am pretty sure we have all asked someone for their advice, however, if you are taking responsibility for your life, then you listen to advice and then decide if this advice is best for you. I am a strong believer of investigating all your options. Sure, ask your parents, friends, spouses, neighbors, or mentor for advice and suggestions, but if you are taking responsibility for your life, you will make the ultimate choice of what is best for you—not what is best for anyone else. Most people like to please their loved ones, but remember, you have to please yourself first.

Everyone wants to feel that they have a say in what happens in their lives. When you do not have a say, you get angry, frustrated, sad, or depressed. You feel hopeless, fearful, and lonely. Imagine if you went to your doctor today and he told you that you have a terminal illness and have six months to live. The first thing you may feel is anger ("How dare he tell me that I only have six months to live?"). You have fear, due to not knowing what to expect. You feel helpless and hopeless, and of course you have feelings of loneliness if you feel alone in this situation. You have no control over what will happen, but you do have control over how you are going to deal with this information, how you are going to spend the rest of your life, and how you are going to treat those around you. Can you imagine if every day, you felt you had no choices and you were totally dependent on others—others are making decisions for your life. How would this make you feel? Just imagine … be honest with yourself. And then ask yourself if you are dependent on someone—and what you can do to change this.

Addiction

By not taking responsibility for your life, you may become addicted to unhealthy substances, such as alcohol, drugs, sex, food, money, and other people. When this occurs you, are not taking responsibility for your life. You are allowing another force to control you and take a dangerous direction with your life.

Within the population that I work with, illegal substances and alcohol abuse takes control of many lives. In 2005, an estimated 22 million Americans struggled with a drug or alcohol problem. Almost 95 percent of people with substance use problems are considered unaware of their problem. Substance abuse has a major impact on individuals, families, and communities. The effects of substance abuse are cumulative, significantly contributing to costly social, physical, mental, and public health problems. These problems include:

Teenage pregnancy
Human immunodeficiency virus/acquired immunodeficiency
    syndrome (HIV/AIDS)
Other sexually transmitted diseases (STDs)
Domestic violence
Child abuse

I am bored and I am TIRED of it!!

Motor vehicle crashes
Physical fights
Crime
Homicide
Suicide

Ninety-nine percent of these individual report that they use substances to numb their hurt, anger, and feelings. They say that substances make them feel numb to the world. Over half of substance abusers have experienced abuse in their past. They *decided* that they are not worthy of having a healthy and happy life, and they give up and want to feel numb. I say they decided because if you are using any illegal substance or drinking alcohol, you make the decision to use this drug. No one puts a pipe to your mouth and makes you use drugs. If you are a substance abuser, you made the decision to use a mind-altering substance. If you drink alcohol to a point that it changes your personality or causes problems in your life, you made the choice of taking that drink. Yes, I understand that it helps you forget reality and feel less stressed, but reality will be here whether you're on drugs or you are not. Reality will never go away. Making the decision to not use substances or to stop using substances has to be your choice, and you will have to take the consequences of this choice. I've mentioned that I smoked marijuana in my teens and early twenties. I now drink alcohol socially, but I was always afraid to try cocaine, methamphetamines, LSD, opiates, or prescription drugs, because I was afraid that I would like it, and then I would want to continue to use it and a cycle would begin. Don't put yourself in this position. Do not set yourself up for failure and become addicted to a substance that will change your life forever.

Addiction to food is a substance to which I can relate. I love food, and I love to eat, especially chocolate. If I could eat chocolate all day and night and not gain a pound, I would. But I know that I cannot do this. Do I have my moments of weakness? Absolutely. Do I get mad at myself for this weakness? Absolutely, but I also know that when this weakness occurs, I have to make amends with it, learn from it, and then move on. Food is like a drug for many. Over 69 percent of the population is overweight or obese. Unlike illegal substances and alcohol, we need to eat to nourish our bodies. I believe, however, that due to this mind-set, we have to eat to survive, we think we can eat and eat and eat and justify this behavior. When you allow your food intake and weight to control your life, then you have a problem with your diet. It is very simple: if you are obese and food controls your life, you have a problem that you need to control. You are not controlling the food; food is controlling you. You are the one who makes the choice to eat three or four hamburgers instead of one. You are the person who chooses to eat a whole chocolate bar or a whole bag of chips. No one else is making you do it.

In a recent study, lab rats fed chocolate treats produced higher levels of a chemical called encephalin, which is linked to the pleasure and reward systems of the brain, much like if you are doing drugs, which in turns makes you feel better. How many times have you gorged yourself with food and felt horrible, full, or bloated, but then do it again and again? Why? That is what you need to ask yourself. If you are overweight and are unable to work, exercise, or take care of your family, then you are allowing food to control your life. You are killing yourself with the choice of eating the extra hamburger or candy bar or bag of chips. Think about this fact, and ask yourself the following questions before you take another bite of food that you know is not healthy for you:

Do I want to eat this?
Do I need to eat this?
How will I feel after I eat?

Then make a choice between the need and want. We all want chocolate, but we do not need it. We all need to eat, but what we eat is the difference between being healthy or obese. You have a choice of what you eat. We have a choice of exercising and keeping your body moving. Exercise is very rewarding—mentally and physically rewarding. I have found that when I exercise on a regular basis, I feel better, emotionally and physically. I am not sure if this is due to my feeling good due to the exercise or because

I am actually getting up and doing something instead of sitting on the couch, being bored. Even walking my dog around the block makes a difference. If you have not been exercising, I suggest you start taking baby steps to making exercise a daily routine. If you have to park farther away from the store to get a walk in, do this. If you have to take a flight of stairs instead of the elevator, do it. If you can find a friend or neighbor to walk around the block, try it out. Just get yourself moving and active. Take notice of how this activity makes you feel. At first, you may be sore, but work through it. Trust me: it will get better.

When you do not take responsibility for yourself, you may become emotionally or physically unhealthy. It surprises me how many people do not go to the doctor or hospital when they are not feeling well due to the fear that they will be diagnosed with a terrible illness. This fear causes people to not take responsibility for their health, which could have long-term consequences. It is just as important for you to take care of your medical issues as it is for you to take care of your emotional needs. Do not ignore those aches, pains, lumps, ongoing sniffles, headaches, backaches, rashes, odors, discolored mole, discharges, or any other medical concerns. The earlier you get a medical concern diagnosed, the better the chance will be that it will not become something serious or life-threatening.

Unable to Develop Trust or to Feel Secure with Others

When you have experienced trauma and/or abuse by a person that you love and trust, it could enable you to not trust or feel secure with this person. Trust issues can begin as early as birth. The first stage of Erik Erikson's model is trust vs. mistrust. As a baby, you cry when you need food, soothing, change of diaper, and care, but if your needs are not met, then you develop distrust of others to satisfy your needs. You learn that when you need something, you cannot not rely on others to help you. You learn not to trust others and are unable to feel secure. The inability to trust others can cause multiple problems. We need to have relationships with others—family members, friends, coworkers, loved ones, and spouses. The one key element to relationships is trust. Without trust and acceptance of another person, a relationship will be weak and unfulfilled.

How many times have you had a falling out in a relationship and felt sad, upset, angry, frustrated, and depressed? When we fail in a relationship, we feel horrible and feel like a failure. Due to this failure we begin to feel that we are unable to love and care for others. We feel that we are unsuccessful in personal relationships. In actuality, we are not failures, and we are able to love others. We just need to learn to trust. You may ask yourself, "How can I trust a person when every person that I trust has disappointed me?" This is not any easy task. I have a hard time trusting my husband because every male figure in my life that I trusted has disappointed me. My father committed suicide; my brother has a hard time being there for others; my ex-husband cheated on me and lied. I am carrying all these trust issues with me against men, and I am trying to have a healthy relationship with my husband. The first thing I needed to do with my current husband was explain these trust issues and make him understand that when I say I don't trust him, it is not that I personally don't trust him; I don't trust men in general. Second, I had to look into myself and recognize these issues so that I can understand them and relate them to my everyday life. Third, I have to recognize these trust issues when they creep into my life and identify them before I overreact.

You should not be naive about others and situations that do not seem right, but recognize them, and make sure you react to real issues and not issues you have created in your head. Then react in a way that will make you feel dignified and heard; this will help you to have a healthy relationship with others and also feel more secure about yourself and your feelings.

Before taking any type of action, ask yourself, "What could be the consequence of my doing this?" If you cannot handle the consequences or the reality of the situation, then don't do it. If you feel that you can handle the consequences, then at least you know what you are getting yourself into.

When we do not take responsibility, we have irrational beliefs about ourselves and about our lives. Irrational beliefs have no justification—we make them up in our heads. As humans, we are wonderfully creative in making up these beliefs to justify our hurt feelings. These irrational beliefs, however, can make us bitter, angry, unproductive, and depressed. Some of the most common irrational beliefs are:

It's not my fault. I am the way I am.
Life is unfair! There is no reason to try.
I am just like my parents.
I will never be able to change.
No one will love me. I am ugly and worthless.
I can't find a good job because I am stupid.
My mom was on welfare, so I will have to be on welfare.
I don't know any better.
I grew up poor. I will always be poor.
All men are alike—liars, cheaters, and worthless
I can only take one hit of crack cocaine; I am cured (addicts).
I can drink one beer; it won't kill me (alcoholics).
I don't need anyone in my life. I can do it all by myself.
Everyone in my family is fat, so I will also be fat.
I can't ...

When we do not take responsibility for our lives, we have these beliefs, and we give up and do not try to improve our life. ("Why should I, when ...?") These beliefs are detrimental to our lives and can cause a lot of heartache and failure. If you have any of these thoughts or any other negative thoughts about yourself, ask yourself (or someone close to you) if these thoughts sound rational or irrational. You need to assess your daily thoughts and be honest with yourself. Ask yourself if you really believe these thoughts, and if so, why.

After my divorce, I had the irrational thought that all men were liar and cheaters. This was definitely a short phase due to my being hurt. I know that this was an irrational belief, because I have male friends who are loyal and fantastic. Due to my experience and hurt feelings, however, I wanted to believe this to justify what happened to me. Fortunately, I was able to recognize this as an irrational belief and change, allowing me to be open to a new relationship. I was able to trust again and have a healthy relationship with my current husband. I cannot say that this thought does not come in my mind every once in a while when a friend is going through what I did, but I know this thought is not true or healthy. You have to be careful with irrational beliefs. If you have thoughts and beliefs that you question and do not have true facts, then you may want to discuss them with someone to get clarity.

Defense Mechanisms

We create defense mechanisms to protect ourselves from being hurt or disappointed, to protect ourselves from negative events or feelings. According to Wikelpedia, *defence mechanisms are unconscious coping mechanisms that reduce anxiety generated by threats from unacceptable impulses. Defence mechanisms, which are unconscious, are not to be confused with conscious coping strategies.* Coping strategies are healthy defense mechanism that when used appropriately and not excessively can help us deal with conflicting or stressful situations. Coping stratgies can include patience, humor, gratitude, acceptance, humility, courage, being mindful and being able to forgive.

There are healthy and unhealthy defense mechanisms that we all have used. I want to focus on some of the defense mechanisms that could become unhealthy if excessively used to protect yourself, causing you to avoid taking responsibility for your actions, thoughts, and feelings.

Denial is when a person is faced with a fact that is too uncomfortable to accept and rejects it instead, insisting that it is not true, despite what may be overwhelming evidence. Denial is the most commonly used defense mechanism to help protect ourselves from the truth. Women may be in denial about their children's bad behavior because it makes them feel less as a mother. Addicts may be in denial about their addiction to avoid having to be clean and sober. People with health issues may be in denial about their diagnosis due to fear of dying. People may be in denial about their behavior to avoid consequences. Denial is a defense mechanism that needs to be recognized, acknowledged, and changed. When we are in denial, we are not being truthful and honest with ourselves, which prevents us from taking responsibility for our actions, thoughts, and feelings.

Dissociation refers to separation or postponement of a feeling that normally would accompany a situation or thought. You are able to totally separate yourself from a situation in order to protect yourself from negative thoughts or feelings. An example of dissociation is when a person is being abused, he or she is able to mentally leave the situation in order not to deal with this emotionally. You are actually able to mentally be in a different place to avoid what is occurring to you. The problem with dissociation is that these memories will continue to haunt you. Usually when you dissociated yourself, you repress these memories and emotions in the subconscious. These memories and emotions will need to be addressed eventually, especially if you are having issues or concerns in your life that are causing you to not move forward and have a successful life.

Regression is the reversion to an earlier stage of development in the face of unacceptable impulses. Have you ever seen adults throw a temper tantrum when they did not get their way? They are no longer acting like adults; they have regressed back to the behavior they used when they were younger. With regression, people learned a behavior that worked for them when they were younger—screaming, crying, manipulating, withdrawing—and more than likely they got what they wanted when they acted this way. As an adult, however, this behavior looks pretty silly and childish. This person is regressing into childlike behavior to get what he/she wants. This is a learned behavior and if not recognized and changed, it can become a terrible habit. More than likely this behavior will not be socially accepted at work, in an adult relationship, with adult friends, and within society.

Projection is attributing to others your own unacceptable or unwanted thoughts and/or emotions. When we are unhappy, we like to make others feel unhappy. When we are rude or nasty to people, we feel like other people are rude or nasty. We like to project our feelings and emotions onto other people. Usually, when we are doing something wrong, we will project this on another person. For example, if a person is cheating on his spouse, he will accuse his spouse of cheating. If a person is using illegal substances, she may accuse her spouse or child of using illegal substances. They try to project whatever they are doing wrong on others to mask their own behavior. You may be mad at your spouse; instead of talking to your spouse about being mad, you go to work and take it out on your coworkers. You are projecting your emotions or actions to the wrong person to avoid taking responsibility of your emotions or actions to the right person. You are blaming others for what you have not accomplished. Projections can be damaging to your thought process and to others.

Repression is the process of pulling thoughts into the unconscious and preventing painful or dangerous thoughts from entering consciousness. The painful feelings are initially conscious and then forgotten. They are stored in the unconscious and, under certain circumstances, can be retrieved. Repression can range from momentary memory lapses to complete amnesia of a catastrophic event, such as a murder or an earthquake. People want to forget painful memories. Repression is a way for your brain to protect you from a traumatic event, but this event will have to be remembered and dealt with. Repressed thoughts can cause multiple issues in your life.

When I was in graduate school, one of my peers was having a difficult time in his marriage. He explained that his wife had a nervous breakdown and was threatening to leave him. Neither he nor his wife understood why she was having a difficult time—he said they had a good marriage and two healthy children, ages five and seven years old. His wife, who had always been a good mother, started distancing herself from the children and stated several times that she did not want to be a mother anymore. She admitted herself in an in-patient psychiatric facility. While in therapy, she started to have memories of being sexually abused by her stepfather around the age of five. She had completely forgotten about this abuse. When her children turned the same age as she was when she was abused, she started to have severe anxiety about being a mother, which caused her to have a nervous breakdown. This is how repressed thoughts can affect you. Even when you are unaware of a situation, your body still reacts to it.

Rationalization is a defense mechanism in which perceived controversial behaviors or feelings are logically justified and explained in a rational or logical manner in order to avoid any true explanation. You are justifying your behavior in your mind to make you feel like it is okay to act a certain way. We all like to rationalize our thoughts and behavior to make them appear the way we want them to appear. I can rationalize my impulsive behavior of eating chocolate all day long, but when I really acknowledge the behavior, I admit it is not good for me or my health. An addict can rationalize that he can take "one more hit" and will not need another because he has beat his addiction. A driver can rationalize that she has to speed or she will be late to work. When you rationalize your negative behaviors, you put yourself at risk of doing actions that are not good for you, which will cause you to not be happy with yourself. You are pretty much fooling yourself. When you rationalize a behavior, you have to ask yourself why you are doing this behavior and if you are going to be okay with the consequence from this behavior. For example, I always tell my clients that if they can rationalize that they can take "one hit" and be okay, then they have to first "play the script" of what will happen if they can't take one hit and relapse in their addiction. If they are okay with how this script is going to play out, then go for it, but again, don't fool yourself into thinking that you are going to stop with that one hit. Also, don't think you are fooling others.

Some clients rationalize their behaviors to me, and I wonder who they think they are fooling—me or themselves. Sometime I will ask them if they think what they said sounded reasonable and logical. Sometimes I will ask them if they think I am stupid to believe what they've said is real. Sometimes I just let them believe their irrational thoughts, because they have rationalized them so much, there is nothing I can say or do to stop them. Usually, we will talk about it later when they have come to the realization that what they did was not in their best interest.

We all have defense mechanisms that we use to protect ourselves from being hurt, emotionally and mentally; however, if you do not recognize these defense mechanisms and continue to have the same problems over and over again, you need to do a self-assessment and determine how using defense mechanisms is affecting your ability to acknowledge and change a certain behavior. If you keep getting the same negative results from your behavior, you have to change your behavior. Try to determine if you are using defense mechanisms in an unhealthy way. Then you will have to determine how you are going to change your behavior and thought process regarding the way you have been using the mechanism. Finally, make a decision on whether this mechanism is really helping you or hurting you.

Chapter 9

How You Can Take Responsibility for Your Life

> *Failure is success if we learn from it.*
> —Malcolm Forbes

You are responsible for determining who you are and what *you* are going to do with your life. *No one* has the authority to make you believe something that you feel and believe is not true. If you do believe irrational thoughts about yourself or about a situation you are in, then they will come true, but if you do not believe them and want to make changes in your life, change will happen. For example if you believe your cannot get a college degree, then more than likely you will not pursue getting a degree, change will not happen. But if you believe you can get your degree, you will make it happen.

Accepting that you can make changes in your life is the first step in taking responsibility and moving forward toward your dreams and wishes.

The next step is not blaming others for the choices you have made in your life. Point the finger back to you when discussing the consequences of your choice and action. Every choice and action you make in your life has consequences—positive or negative. Always learn from these consequences and make a conscious effort not to do the same negative behavior over and over again.

The third step is not allowing fear and shame to stop you. Once you know what you want, and you can envision accomplishing what you want, the next step is overcoming the fear and shame and moving forward. Getting out of your rut and comfort zone will be difficult, but it can be done.

Realizing that you determine your feelings about any events or actions addressed to you, no matter how negative they seem, will allow you to address your negative feeling. It also will allow you to move forward instead of staying stuck in that negative feeling. Don't allow yourself to forget the negative feelings, but allow yourself to move forward. So many times, grief overcomes a person. Allow yourself to grieve for a specific time, but then you will have to move forward in your life and not become stuck in grief and sadness. If you are grieving the loss of someone special, realize that person would not want you to allow his or her death to overcome your life and stop you from living.

Do not feel sorry for the "bum deal" you have been handed, but take hold of your life and give it direction and reason. It is how you deal with a bad situation that matters. Let go of blame and anger toward those in your past; let go of regrets and should have, could have and would haves, because your past will never change, but your future can.

Realize that you cannot control what is going to occur, you cannot control what another person is going to do, and you cannot control what others think or feel about you. You can only control how *you* react to them and how *you* will let them affect your life. You should have control over your life. You should be the person driving your car in the direction you want it to go and not allowing the backseat drivers to tell you where you should go. You have the ability to know yourself and what you want from your life.

Throughout this book, I have had you ask yourself questions, and I hope that you have been able to be truthful with yourself when answering so that you can get to the root of what you want from your life. We know that we need to take responsibility for our lives and actions, but how many of us are actually doing that?

Remember to take care of yourself, physically and emotionally. Take care of your body by exercising, moving, eating healthily, going for doctor appointments, and making sure you are "right" with yourself.

Be honest with yourself and with others. There is a saying: the truth will set you free—but will it? If you are truthful with yourself and can honestly admit your strengths and your weaknesses and honestly admit who you are, the truth will set you free. However, if you admit all your faults and weaknesses to others, will it really set you free? That is the question you have to ask yourself—how truthful do you want to be with others? How truthful can you be with others about yourself and still feel loved and respected?

During one of my substance-abuse groups, I asked about thirty individuals, who are addicted to pain medication and other drugs, to describe themselves. None of them described himself or herself as an addict—no one! When asked why they did not, many stated, "That is a given; I am in this group." Some did not believe that they were addicts, even though they admitted to abusing drugs over and over again. Some did not want to categorize themselves as addicts, due to not currently using substances. Some explained that they did not like to tell others they were addicts due to the stigma. I explained to them that the group setting was the place to admit that they were addicts, "you don't have to hide behind a mask in this group, because everyone is an addict, this is the one place where you can be honest and vulnerable about your addiction". As the group members talked about who they were, it became clear that most of these individuals did not know who they were and were not being honest with themselves. They were hiding behind what they thought they should be or what they wanted people to think of them.

So it got me thinking about how honest these individuals were about who they really are. I explained to them that without being honest with themselves, they could not be honest with others. How can you move forward in your life if you are unable to admit your faults and the ugly truths about you? At least be honest with yourself, and then determine who you really need to be honest with and why.

Use "I" statements instead of "you" statements. I have had to do a lot of self-actualization due to having the wonderful habit of blaming others for the choices I have made. I love to use the "you" word when telling another person what he or she has done to make me unhappy. I have learned to use the "I" word when discussing my feelings. Yes, I know that it is easier to blame others for our feelings, and yes, it makes us feel better when we take the responsibility off ourselves when we are hurt and angry. In the long run, however, it does not fix the hurt feelings, and it does not make the problem go away.

Using the word "you" instead of "I" is a way of taking away the responsibility from you and placing it on others. This allows you to talk about your experiences and focus on how another person's actions or experiences have affected you. When using the "I" statement, it places responsibility back to you and your experiences. It gives others a chance to see how you feel, how you interpreted an action, how you interpreted what was being said, or how you viewed a situation. When using "I" statements, you speak from your own experiences, and this allows you to justify your feelings, emotions, actions, and choices in an effective communication manner. Every day, I struggle with this in my relationship with my husband. I like to say, "You are not making me happy" or "You need to work around the house more instead of playing golf." After making these statements, my husband would, of course, become defensive and make statements such as, "I guess I can't make you happy. Why don't you find another husband?" or "What do you do around the house?" After having these conversations a zillion times, I realized that my stating "you" instead of "I" was not going to make our relationship any better. I began to choose my words wisely when talking to my husband about the feelings that I was having. Instead of stating, "You are not making me happy," I used, "I am not happy about …" Or "I am happy when you do …" When expressing my feeling toward my husband's playing golf, instead of stating, "You are always playing golf and not doing chores around the house," I would state, "I would appreciate it if you did not play golf today and helped me take care of the chores around the house."

I asked my husband for feedback about the difference between these statements and how they came across to him. He stated that he felt less defensive when I used "I" statements and also felt that he could make comments on these statements in a positive manner. I felt more empowered by taking ownership of my feelings and actions and not relying on another person to justify my feelings, action, and thoughts.

Making changes in our communication styles can be challenging; it can take a long time to get the hang of it. I still find it a challenge and catch myself stating "you" instead of "I." However, I can tell immediately, when I use "you" instead of "I" when talking to my husband. This one simple change in communication can open up new possibilities of taking responsibility for my actions and life.

Being empowered and having self-respect and confidence in yourself can make a world of difference. Taking responsibility for your life is empowering and allows you to feel good about yourself and your life. *Empowerment* is when you feel and have power and control over your life. It is a feeling of accomplishment, high self-esteem, and confidence that allows you to feel that you have control and choices in your life. This is a wonderful feeling; you should feel it when you think about your life. I worked with a woman who was in an abusive relationship. She felt hopeless about her life and felt that her only choice was to stay in this relationship, remain homeless, and remain dependent on substances. After discussing with this woman the positive choices she could make— she had three really good choices—she realized that she did not need to remain in this abusive relationship and could get the help she needed. Two days later, this particular woman came to me and used the word "empowered." She explained that she was ready to leave her boyfriend and go into a substance-abuse treatment program and fix herself. We were able to get this woman enrolled into a program that day. She stated that it felt good to realize that she did have choices that gave her a sense of empowerment and control of her life. Remember, everyone has choices—either to go right or left. You are responsible for the direction in your life. Once you are able to recognize this and act on it, you will succeed.

Respect for yourself and getting respect from others is a choice that everyone can make, no matter what situation they are in. You can be in a pile of shit, but with self-respect and respect for others, it will appear you are in a pool of roses. Respect for yourself is the key to good self-esteem and confidence. Respect for yourself means that you will not want to do anything that is against your morals, values, and beliefs. For example, I always preach self-respect to adolescent females who are participating or thinking about participating in sexual activity. I tell them to have respect for their bodies and actions. My nieces have especially heard me tell them to have self-respect, especially with boys and sex. Self-respect is having the confidence and security to keep your head high and look at others, eye to eye.

Respect others. You don't have to like a person, but you may have to respect him or her. This usually has to do with bosses, coworkers, and family members. You do not have to respect their actions or decisions, but you do have to respect their position and who they are. You can't blow up at everyone who disagrees with you. You may not like it, but you have to respect their opinions and differences. In today's society, it seems that everyone is supposed to feel and think the same way, and when you voice your own opinion, which may disagree with others, you are considered bad, a racist, or a bigot, when in actuality you are just giving your opinion. In America, we are supposed to be able to do this without judgment and consequences, but this does not seem to occur anymore. Taking responsibly for your thoughts, decisions, and actions is the first step toward knowing how you feel toward a certain situation and being able to stand for your beliefs. Doing this in a respectful, nonviolent manner is the best way to express yourself and allow others to recognize that it is okay if you don't agree or have the same opinion. Treat those around you the way you want to be treated—this is respect.

Everyone experiences boredom. Remember, there is nothing wrong with being bored from time to time. By taking responsibility for your life and not allowing your body and mind to be bored and useless on a continuing basis, you are allowing yourself to continue to grow and blossom. You are allowing yourself to make decisions in your life that will give you purpose and meaning. Continue to set goals in your life and want more for yourself.

After reading this book, I hope you find that you have choices to get help regarding depression, trauma, anxiety, obesity, and boredom. Take control of your life instead of allowing these issues to control you. Keep busy, and more important, keep being honest with yourself. You are only fooling yourself if you continue to ignore those nagging thoughts that keep you up at night. I recommend that you go back and answer the questions that are in this book. Some questions will be harder to answer than others. Focus on these questions, because these likely are the questions that you are struggling with. The key to making changes is recognizing the behaviors, thoughts, and feelings that you want to change and making a *conscious* effort to make these changes. Allow yourself to live the life you want to truly live and continue to live and learn.